PEOPLE OF
THE FUR TRADE

From Native Trappers to Chief Factors

IRENE TERNIER GORDON

VICTORIA · VANCOUVER · CALGARY

Heritage House Publishing Company Ltd.
www.heritagehouse.ca

Library and Archives Canada Cataloguing in Publication
Gordon, Irene Ternier
People of the fur trade: from native trappers to chief factors / Irene Ternier Gordon.

(Amazing stories)
Includes bibliographical references and index.
Issued also in an electronic format.
ISBN 978-1-926936-92-5

1. Fur traders—Canada—Biography. 2. Fur trade—Canada—History. 3. Northwest, Canadian—History. I. Title. II. Series: Amazing stories (Victoria, B.C.)

FC3212.1.A1G67 2011   971.2'01092   C2011-905034-X

Series editor: Lesley Reynolds.
Proofreader: Liesbeth Leatherbarrow.
Cover design: Chyla Cardinal. Interior design: Frances Hunter.
Cover photo: "Trading Post" by C.W. Jeffreys, Library and Archives Canada C-073431.

The interior of this book was printed on 100% post-consumer recycled paper, processed chlorine free and printed with vegetable-based inks.

Heritage House acknowledges the financial support for its publishing program from the Government of Canada through the Canada Book Fund (CBF), Canada Council for the Arts and the province of British Columbia through the British Columbia Arts Council and the Book Publishing Tax Credit.

15 14 13 12 11   1 2 3 4 5
Printed in Canada

*To my parents, Gaston Ternier and Helen D'Hondt, and
to the memory of my Ternier and D'Hondt grandparents, who
were founders of Canadian farm and garden families rather
than fur-trade families. Also, I dedicate this book to my siblings
Jim, Betty and Judy, who continue in the family tradition
to the present day.*

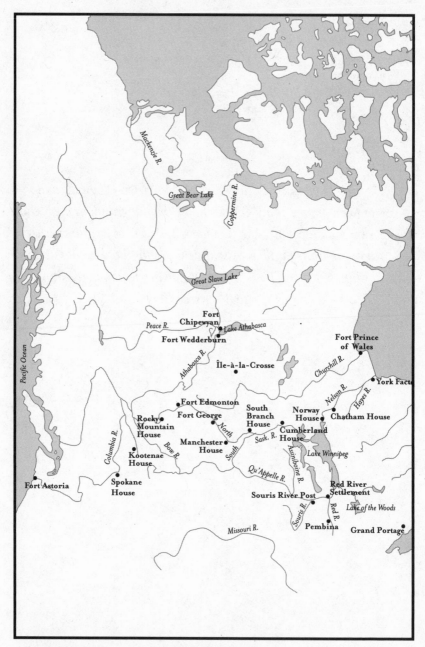

This map shows many of the major trading posts, lakes and rivers used by the fur trade between 1763 and 1821.

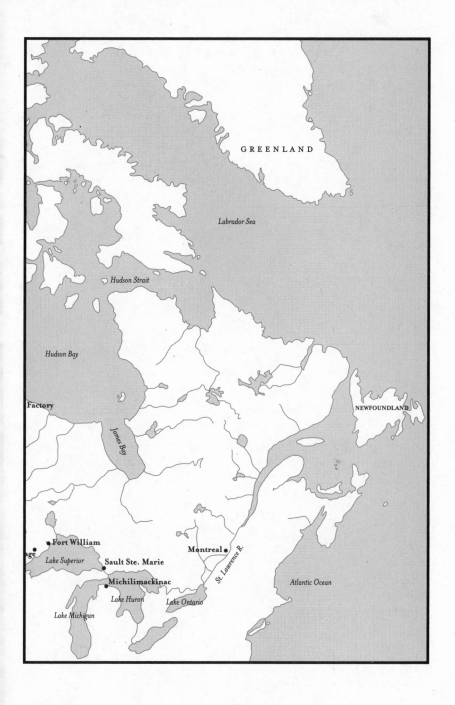

Contents

Prologue

ON JUNE 2, THE OJIBWA *announced that they were going to celebrate the king's birthday on June 4 by playing a game of lacrosse (or baggataway, as it is known to the Ojibwa) against the neighbouring Sacs for a high wager. Everyone at Fort Michilimackinac was invited to the game. Even the fort's commander accepted the invitation, and he "only smiled" at Alexander Henry's suspicions of the Ojibwa's motives. Henry did not go to the game and spent the afternoon writing letters.*

As lacrosse is attended with much violence and noise, nothing would be less liable to excite alarm than to have the ball tossed over the fort wall, with all the players following after it. Suddenly, Henry heard loud noises "of general confusion." Rushing to his window, he saw Ojibwa rushing into the fort and "*furiously cutting down and scalping every Englishman they found.*"

Henry snuck out of his house and over to his Canadian next-door neighbours, where the servant girl hid him in the attic. Finally, he heard shouts of, "All is finished." At the same instant, some Ojibwa entered the house where he was hiding and demanded to know if there were any Englishmen there. The neighbour replied that they might look for themselves if they wished. The servant had locked the door into the attic after hiding Henry, so he had a few moments to hide in a heap of birchbark maple-sugar containers before the door opened. Four blood-smeared men armed with tomahawks entered and looked around. They did not immediately see Henry in the dark attic, but would they search more carefully?

Introduction

FROM THE FIRST MEETING BETWEEN Europeans and Native North Americans, the fur trade defined Canadian history. The story of the Canadian West, in particular, is the story of the fur trade. One of the most important and exciting periods of fur-trade history was the almost 60 years between the fall of New France to Britain in 1763 and the 1821 amalgamation of the Hudson's Bay and North West companies.

The Hudson's Bay Company (HBC) came into existence in 1670 when it received a British Royal Charter from King Charles II granting it control over all lands draining into Hudson Bay. In modern terms, that includes northern Quebec and Ontario, Manitoba, Saskatchewan, southern

Alberta and parts of the Northwest Territories. This land was officially named Rupert's Land in honour of the king's cousin Prince Rupert, who was named first governor of the HBC, but it was commonly referred to as the North-West.

The HBC began by trading furs from posts on the shores of Hudson and James bays. Its employees, who were mainly recruited from England or Scotland's Orkney Islands, often referred to it as the Honourable Company. Some northerners, however, joked more recently that HBC stood for "Here before Christ," an indication of the power wielded by the HBC from its formation well into the 20th century.

The North West Company (NWC), based in Montreal, began as a fur-trading syndicate in the late 1770s. Most of the partners were Scottish Highlanders, and their employees were largely other Highlanders, Canadians and Métis. During the period covered by this book, the term "Canadian" referred only to someone of French descent who had been born in Quebec or Lower Canada. The Métis, off-spring of the original fur traders and First Nations women, became the largest single group involved in the fur trade.

This book tells the history of the fur trade between 1763 and 1821 through the lives of people who represent the trade's many occupations and ethnic groups. Both the HBC and the NWC were hierarchical companies. The HBC was headed by a governor and committee based in England, which set company policy. Factors, the men in charge of the posts or factories in North America, were responsible

Introduction

for implementing company policy and supervising employees, who ranged from skilled tradesmen to labourers, called servants. Native people living near the HBC posts became known as the Homeguard Cree. In addition to working as trappers, some of the Homeguard were hired as hunters to help feed the traders, or acted as middlemen between the HBC and First Nations people living farther away from the posts.

At the top of the North West Company hierarchy were a small number of partners based in Montreal. The Montreal partners, the wintering partners who managed the wilderness posts and the salaried clerks were known as the bourgeois. They were considered gentlemen, unlike the engagés or labourers.

This book also includes a map showing the major trading posts and waterways, a fur-trade timeline and a bibliography for readers who would like more detailed information.

CHAPTER

1

The Great Lakes Traders

Your king has never sent us any presents, nor entered into any treaty with us. Wherefore he and we are still at war . . . [but] you come in peace, to trade with us . . . We shall regard you, therefore, as a brother, and you may sleep tranquilly.

—CHIEF MINAVAVANA TO
ALEXANDER HENRY THE ELDER

Alexander Henry Begins His Fur-Trade Career

Alexander Henry the Elder should not be confused with his nephew, Alexander Henry the Younger, who was also a well-known fur trader. Both men wrote important accounts of their experiences in the fur trade. Henry the Elder considered himself an Englishman, despite being born in New Jersey. He began his career as a merchant supplying the British army during the French and Indian War. (This was the North American part of the Seven Years War, in which the British fought against the French and their Native allies.) Henry was with General Jeffrey Amherst when Amherst captured Montreal. On their way to Montreal, Amherst's forces suffered a serious accident in some rapids, losing nearly 100 men and a quantity of military stores and provisions. Henry, who lost three boatloads of merchandise, spent several hours trapped in one of his boats, which luckily had run aground on some rocks, before he was finally rescued.

Following the fall of New France to the British in 1763, the area opened to English traders. Henry, after hearing of the trade possibilities at Michilimackinac, decided to go there. He applied to the governor of Montreal, who, according to Henry, "very reluctantly" granted him permission. Because no peace treaty had yet been signed between the English and the First Nations peoples, the governor was "apprehensive that both the property and the lives of his majesty's subjects would be very insecure."

Henry Arrives at Michilimackinac

As he travelled to Michilimackinac, Henry exchanged his English clothes for the dress of a Canadian voyageur, smeared his face and hands with dirt and grease and took the place of one of his canoemen. Whenever a strange canoe approached, he used the paddle with as much skill as he possessed. No one paid the slightest attention to him.

The disguise was necessary because of an incident that had taken place at a village he visited on his way from Montreal to Michilimackinac, a fort located on the Straits of Mackinac connecting Lakes Huron and Michigan. At first the villagers had been friendly, and Henry traded some small articles for fish and dried meat. When they discovered that he was not a Canadian, however, they demanded a keg of rum because, they argued, he would certainly be killed at Michilimackinac and "they had a right to a share of the pillage."

The people of Michilimackinac were Ojibwa (called Chippewa by the Americans), members of the largest group of First Nations people in Canada. Those who later moved to the Prairies became known as Saulteaux because they originally lived around Sault Ste. Marie.

Most First Nations people had supported the French or Canadians against the British during the French and Indian War, which had ended with the capitulation of New France to the British in September 1760. Henry's men suggested that he disguise himself as a Canadian voyageur for the remainder of his trip to Michilimackinac to avoid any more confrontations. Once Henry arrived in Michilimackinac, he put his goods in the hands of his assistant, and the two men agreed that the assistant "should pass for the proprietor."

Not surprisingly, Henry's secret was soon out. Chief Minavavana called upon him with a delegation of about 60 men, marching in single file, "each with his tomahawk in one hand and scalping knife in the other." Most were bare-chested, except for a few who had blankets over their shoulders. Their faces were painted with charcoal mixed with grease and their bodies with white clay. Some had decorated their heads and noses with feathers. Minavavana entered Henry's house first, followed by the other men, who silently sat down on the floor on a signal from the chief. Minavavana was six feet tall with "an indescribable mixture of good and evil" showing in his face, according to Henry. The chief began by observing that the English must be brave men who were not afraid of death since Henry had dared to come among his enemies. Then Minavavana fell silent, and the men gravely smoked their pipes while Henry "inwardly endured the tortures of suspense." Finally, Minavavana began his official speech:

> Englishman, it is to you that I speak and I demand your attention! Englishman, you know that the French king is our father. He promised to be such, and we in return promised to be his children . . . Englishman, it is you that have made war with this our father . . . [and] you are his enemy. Your king has never sent us any presents, nor entered into any treaty with us. Wherefore he and we are still at war . . . [but] you come in peace, to trade with us . . . We shall regard you, therefore, as a brother, and you may sleep tranquilly . . . As a token of our friendship, we present you with this pipe to smoke.

As Minavavana said these words, someone presented Henry with a pipe. He drew in three puffs of smoke. Then the pipe was handed to the chief and afterwards passed around to every man in the room. Following the pipe ceremony, everyone shook hands with Henry.

Convinced by Minavavana's speech of the good will of the Ojibwa, Henry hired Canadian interpreters and clerks to take his trade goods into the surrounding area. Everything was ready for Henry's men to depart when 200 Ottawa warriors from the nearby village of L'Arbre Croche on Lake Michigan arrived. (The Ottawa, or Odawa, who later gave their name to Canada's capital, are related to the Ojibwa and come from the St. Lawrence and Great Lakes areas.) The Ottawa were angry that Henry and several other merchants in the area had not come to their village and evidently did not intend to trade with them. They requested that the traders give each man goods to the value of 50 made beaver (prepared prime beaver pelts, used as a unit of exchange) and promised to pay for the goods the following summer. Henry and his fellow merchants were seriously concerned by this request for two reasons. First, complying would leave them no goods to trade with anyone else. Second—and more serious—the Ojibwa told them that these Ottawa were notorious for not paying their debts. The Ottawa told the traders that they would give them until the next morning to decide what to do, adding that if the merchants rejected their request, they would take the goods by force.

Voyageurs run the rapids on central Ontario's Mattawa River in this engraving from a painting by Frances Anne Hopkins.
PROVINCIAL ARCHIVES OF MANITOBA/HBC ARCHIVES N16859

Early the next morning, the Ottawa called a second council, but the merchants refused to attend and remained holed up in Henry's house. Toward sunset, word arrived that a detachment of British soldiers were on their way to Michilimackinac and would arrive early the next day. The merchants remained on alert the whole night. At daybreak, they were relieved to see the Ottawa preparing to leave. By sunrise, they were all gone. The Canadians, who had avoided all contact with the merchants while the Ottawa were present, now came to report that the Ottawa had suggested that the Canadians and the Ottawa should march out to attack the troops. When the Canadians refused, the Ottawa left. Three hundred soldiers arrived at Michilimackinac at noon, and several days later the merchants decided it was safe to send their canoes out for the winter trade.

Henry Meets the Cadotte Family

Jean-Baptiste Cadotte was a Canadian who had been hired to manage a small fort at Sault Ste. Marie (now in Michigan) in 1750. It was a key point on the water route to the interior because all canoes going between Lakes Huron and Superior had to be portaged or pulled (lined) through these rapids. Cadotte's wife, Athanasie, a highly respected relative of an important Ojibwa chief, was a great asset to her husband. The family spoke Ojibwa at home, and Cadotte's fluency and skill as an orator won him the position of chief of the local band of about 50 warriors. When the British took control of the Sault in 1762, after the fall of Quebec, Cadotte acted as an interpreter for the small military garrison.

After passing the winter of 1761–62 at Michilimackinac, Alexander Henry visited Sault Ste. Marie in the spring. He decided to spend the next winter there because of its pleasant location and in order to learn the Ojibwa language from the Cadotte family. His plans were disrupted by a fire overnight on December 22 that destroyed all of the buildings at the Sault except for Cadotte's house. It also destroyed part of the stockade and most of the winter's provisions. Henry managed to rescue the military commander, who suffered burns, and saved a small amount of gunpowder moments before the fire reached it.

Henry travelled on snowshoes between Michilimackinac and the Sault several times over the winter and spring of 1762–63. On one trip, he suffered from "snowshoe evil," which he described as an inflammation caused by strain on the tendons of the leg. The usual remedy, according to Henry, was to lay a piece of burning wood on the affected part and leave it there until the flesh was burnt to the nerve. Although Henry claimed that he had seen this treatment used successfully on other people, he "did not think proper to make upon myself."

Wawatam

When Alexander Henry arrived back in Michilimackinac in May 1763, he found four other traders had already arrived. They reported that the First Nations people were still hostile to the English, but Michilimackinac seemed fairly safe since the garrison there consisted of 93 men, and the Ojibwa only had small arms as weapons. Large numbers of Ojibwa daily assembled from all directions until there were about 400 around the fort. Although they appeared friendly, Henry felt that "no confidence ought to be placed in them."

Henry had made one good friend among the Ojibwa at Michilimackinac shortly after he first arrived there in 1761. Wawatam was a chief about 45 years old with "an excellent character among his nation." One day, he had arrived with his whole family, bringing a large gift of skins, sugar and dried meat. He made a formal speech, telling Henry that he had observed a fast "in the hope to obtain from the Great Spirit, protection through all his days." During this fast, he had dreamed that he was to adopt an Englishman "as his son, brother and friend." He believed Henry was the man the Great Spirit had chosen for him and hoped that Henry would accept the gift he brought. Henry replied that he would be happy to accept the gift and to have such a good man as Wawatam as a friend and brother.

Now, in early June 1763, Henry and Wawatam met again. Wawatam warned Henry that he was in danger and begged him to leave for Sault Ste. Marie the next day. Henry refused to leave until his clerks arrived back from their winter's trading expedition. The next day, Wawatam returned with his wife and repeated his warning that Henry should leave. Although Henry was able to carry on an ordinary conversation in Ojibwa by this time, he found that Native speech was "so extravagantly figurative" that only someone who had perfectly mastered the language could "comprehend it entirely." Later, he came to believe that had he understood the language better, he might have paid heed to Wawatam's warning and saved himself and others.

A Deadly Lacrosse Game

Everyone at Fort Michilimackinac, with the exception of Henry, apparently accepted the invitation to attend the lacrosse game between the Ojibwa and the Sacs to celebrate the birthday of George III, the British king. Henry excused himself from attending the game by saying that he had letters to write. When he was almost finished his letters, he heard loud noises "of general confusion." Rushing to his window, he saw his worst fears being realized. The Ojibwa were rushing into the fort "furiously cutting down and scalping every Englishman they found." The nearly 300 Canadians also in the fort were looking on, neither opposing nor being injured in the attack. Henry now realized the significance of the Ojibwa's behaviour on the day of Wawatam's visit to him. That day, large numbers of men had come to buy small axes and to look at the silver armbands and other valuable ornaments he had for sale.

Henry escaped detection after the lacrosse game by hiding in his neighbour's attic, but the Ojibwa returned the next morning and told the family that they had not found Henry's body, so he must be hidden somewhere. Fearing that the Ojibwa would take revenge on them, the neighbours confessed that Henry was hidden in their attic but vowed that they had not known he was there the previous day. The Ojibwa immediately took Henry captive. He joined the 20 soldiers and traders who had survived the attack.

Following his capture, Henry lived with Wawatam and his family for almost a year before he returned to Michilimackinac. Life was hard, but it would certainly have been much harder had he not been under Wawatam's protection. Despite his problems, Henry kept his sense of humour. Part of the time he was disguised as an Ojibwa, which required that his head be shaved. He wrote, "I parted, not without some regret, with the long hair . . . which I fancied to be ornamental; but the ladies . . . appeared to think my person improved and now condescended to call me handsome, even among Indians."

When Henry returned to Michilimackinac, his problems were not yet over. Another band of hostile Ojibwa arrived and threatened him. He decided to return to Sault Ste. Marie, where he believed that the Ojibwa were "peacefully inclined." He was wondering how he could reach the Sault when his problem was unexpectedly solved. A canoe under sail arrived, manned by three Canadian voyageurs. It was carrying Madame Cadotte home from Montreal. She agreed to take Henry with her. Again, he disguised himself as a Canadian for safety's sake. The next day, some Ojibwa surrounded Madame Cadotte's canoe and "challenged" Henry as an Englishman. Madame Cadotte assured them that he was a Canadian she was bringing from Montreal, and they reached the Sault safely.

O-Sha-Gush-Ko-Da-Na-Qua

If the Cadottes were the "first family" at Sault Ste. Marie in the 1770s and 80s, that position was held in the next generation by O-Sha-Gush-Ko-Da-Na-Qua (Woman of the Green Glade) and her husband, John Johnston. Green Glade, who became known as Susan after her marriage, was born around 1772 into a prominent Ojibwa family near La Pointe, Wisconsin. She was granddaughter of a war chief who fought with the French at the Plains of Abraham and daughter of Chief Waub-Ojeeg (White Fisher).

Johnston, an upper-class Irishman, arrived in North America about 1791 and became a wintering partner with the NWC. Soon after, he went to La Pointe, where he met Waub-Ojeeg and his daughter. Almost immediately, Johnston asked the chief for permission to marry Green Glade, but Waub-Ojeeg refused. He told Johnston to return to Montreal with his furs and spend the winter there. If the women of Montreal "do not put my child out of your mind, return hither in the spring and we will talk farther," he concluded.

The following spring, Johnston was still determined to marry Green Glade. Before her marriage, she went on a vision quest. She painted herself black and fasted for 10 days while living in a little lodge of cedar boughs on a hill away from everyone. The only person she saw during that time was her grandmother, who came periodically to bring her water. She dreamed continually that a white man accompanied by a dog approached her with a cup in his hand, saying, "Poor thing, why are you punishing yourself? Why do you fast? Here is food for you."

She also dreamed that she was on a high hill surrounded by water with many canoes full of Indians coming to her and paying her homage. Then she was carried into the heavens and could see that the earth was on fire. She feared all her relatives would be burned, but a voice told her that they would be safe.

Finally, she felt satisfied that the white stranger was to be her guardian spirit and returned to her father's lodge. Shortly afterwards, her family married her to Johnston. Despite the dreams she had during her vision quest, she did not wish to marry him and cowered in the corner of his lodge for the first 10 days of her marriage while her husband tried to overcome her fear. Then she ran away. When her father found that she had not behaved properly as a wife, he beat her with a stick and took her back to her husband with a gift of furs and corn. After that, she lived happily with Johnston for 36 years until his death in 1828, according to the story of her courtship and marriage that she and her daughters told to Irish author Anna Brownell Jameson many years later.

As a young woman, Susan was a skilful hunter who "was accounted the surest eye and fleetest foot among the woman of her tribe." During much of her life, she was actively involved in manufacturing maple sugar and in fishing. Every fall, she would fish for about two weeks and preserve the catch for her family's winter food supply, and every spring she would prepare a large amount of maple sugar. She and her son William managed the family's sugaring and fishing businesses after her husband's death and ran the family fur-trading business until 1831.

Peter Pond

Like Alexander Henry, Peter Pond was American-born. He described his family as well-known for five generations as "all warriors either by sea or land." Following the family tradition, he joined the army as a teenager so did not enter the fur trade until he was in his mid-twenties. Pond would undoubtedly have preferred that posterity remember him as a successful explorer and fur trader; however, today he is chiefly known as a man whose career was damaged by his violent temper and his connection with the deaths of three men. His highly idiosyncratic spelling is preserved in this quotation describing the first of the violent deaths with which he was connected during his fur-trading career:

> It hapend that a perons who was in trade himself to abuse me in a shameful manner knowing that if I resented he could shake me in peaces at the same time supposing that I dare not sea him at the pints or at leas I would not. But the abuse was too grate. We met the next morning eairley and discharged pistols in which the pore fellowe was unfortunate. I then came down the countrey and declared the fact. But there was none to prosecute me.

No other details are known about this duel, which he fought with an unnamed man over an unspecified insult shortly after he entered the trade.

Pond formed a partnership with a man named Felix Graham in 1771, trading from New York to Michilimackinac.

Pond described trade at Michilimackinac at the time he arrived there, about 10 years after Alexander Henry:

> Many hundred people . . . [were] trading with the tribes that came a great distance with their furs, skins and maple sugar etc. to market. To those may be added dried venison, bear grease, and the like . . . Other [traders] were employed in making up their equipment . . . to pass the winter with ye Indian tribes and trade what they get from the hunt of ye winter ensuing. I was one of this description. I divided my goods into twelve parts and fitted out twelve large canoes for different parts of the Mississippi River. [spelling corrected]

Although Pond gained a reputation as a hot-tempered man, the following story from his time at Michilimackinac shows him in a somewhat different light. There was no resident priest when Pond was there, but he wrote that missionaries sometimes came for short stays, and that when the traders arrived in spring, the engagés often went to confession. According to Pond, one of his engagés, a young man named Baptiste, "was addicted to thieving" and stole silver trinkets to the value of 10 pounds from him. Baptiste, who had heard good things about the priest, decided to go to confession. He did so, but the priest told him "something was wanting" and would not give him absolution. Baptiste returned to Pond and asked for two otter skins, promising that he would behave better in future and serve him well if he got the skins. Pond gave him the requested skins. Soon after, Baptiste returned. When Pond asked him what had happened, he replied, "Father says my case is a bad one but if I bring two otter more he will take my case on himself and discharge me." Pond gave him two more skins. Not long afterwards, Baptiste returned again. He was, as Pond put it, "as full of thanks as he could express and served me well after."

By the time he returned to Michilimackinac in July 1774, Pond had made enough profit to buy out his partner, Graham. The next year, he headed to the North-West, where he would later begin his connection with the NWC.

CHAPTER

2

Hudson's Bay Men vs. the Canadians

I am certain he hath a secret kindness for his old masters and is not to be depended on. [I told him] that he was doing wrong as he was under a written contract to serve the Company, but all to no purpose.

—MATTHEW COCKING,
SPEAKING OF LOUIS PRIMEAU

Pedlars and Servants

One of the earliest Canadian fur traders in the Saskatchewan River country was Louis Primeau (spelled Primo by the English). Unlike most Canadians, he remained in the North-West during the French and Indian War, gaining much knowledge of First Nations peoples and influence with them. In 1765, the HBC hired Primeau to work as an inland trader. To the fury of the Company, he left for Canada on holiday in 1773 and returned as an employee of a Montreal trading company that was a forerunner to the NWC. Primeau was to play a significant role in the early NWC success against the HBC. Little is known of his later career, but he was likely in charge of Cumberland House in 1798.

Another early meeting between the HBC and Canadian traders in the North-West took place between William Tomison of the HBC and Canadian François Le Blanc (also called Franceways or Saswee) in 1766. Franceways, who had been outfitted with a large cargo of trade goods by Montreal merchants, had enjoyed a successful year of trading. Tomison described him as "a poor looking small man about fifty years of age" but also admitted that Franceways seemed to have great control over his men. Men connected with the NWC were commonly known as Nor'Westers; however, HBC men sneeringly referred to them as "pedlars" and felt themselves superior. Fur-trade historian Marjorie Wilkins Campbell sums up the Canadians' character as "devil-may-care and independent," while the typical HBC man behaved as a "humble-servant-of-a-great-company."

Thomas Corry, one of the first Scottish traders to come from Montreal, arrived in the North-West about 1770. Corry's encroachment on what the HBC considered their territory caused factor Andrew Graham to send an employee named Matthew Cocking inland in 1772. Cocking, who was born in England, was "entertained"—meaning he signed a contract—in 1765 to work as a writer for the HBC for five years at 20 pounds per year. As a writer, he transcribed post journals and correspondence in an elegant hand. Corry's trading proved so successful that he retired to Montreal soon after Cocking met him.

Matthew Cocking Goes Inland

As Matthew Cocking described in his detailed personal journal, his first trip to the interior from York Factory on Hudson Bay had an inauspicious beginning:

> Saturday June 27, 1772—This day at noon took my departure from York Fort . . . The Indians were unwilling to proceed, being such bad weather; and two of them becoming sickly, so we put up for the night, four miles above the Fort.
>
> Monday 29—At 7 AM proceeded, but my canoe mate died; we put up for the night.
>
> Thursday July 2—In the evening a few canoes overtook us [and I] prevailed with one of the natives to make a third person in my canoe.

Not only was illness a problem, but Cocking had little experience as a canoeist when he set out. In his journal, he made it clear that he believed it was urgent that the HBC push their operations inland. It was no longer good enough for them to wait on Hudson Bay for trappers to bring furs to them.

Illness—likely influenza—continued to be a problem for Cocking's expedition until late July. On July 14, he wrote, "Two of our company are sickly, lying helpless in the canoes. One canoe overtook us. They informed us that four Indians are dead." And on July 20, "the labour [lies] heavy on the few healthful people amongst us."

Illness was not the only problem. On July 13, Cocking wrote, "Hungry times: a quarter of an eagle, gull, or duck is one person's allowance per day." Two days later, they reached a lake with plenty of fish, but on July 21 he complained, "I am wearied with fish, eating scarcely anything else." Finally, in August, food became more plentiful and varied. On Sunday, August 2, "Men went a hunting moose, killed one, good food." And on August 21, "Natives killed many red deer."

On August 4, Cocking met a Homeguard Cree from York Factory who denied having traded with the pedlars; however, he had Canadian goods in his possession. The next day, Cocking met 15 canoes of Cree "who had traded all their furs with the pedlars." By late August, he was becoming discouraged and wrote that all the First Nations people he met promised faithfully not to trade with the pedlars next year and to bring their furs to the HBC fort, but he did not believe them. "I find they consider an Englishman's going to them as a person sent to collect furs and not as an encouragement to them to trap furs and come down to the settlements."

Cocking met his first Blackfoot at the end of November. He presented the principal men in a camp of 28 tents with tobacco and other gifts. He wrote:

> I endeavoured to persuade two of them to accompany me on my return to the fort, where they would meet with a hearty welcome and receive many presents, but they said that they would be starved and were unacquainted with canoes and mentioned the long distance. I am certain they never can be prevailed upon to undertake such journeys.

In mid-December, when he had reached a point somewhere west of the Eagle Hills in what is now west-central Saskatchewan, Cocking began his return trip to York Factory. On February 23, he sent presents of tobacco to three Native leaders to try to convince them to accompany him to York Factory, "where they would meet with kind treatment and receive more in return for their furs" than from the Canadians.

Cocking arrived at Franceways' settlement on May 20, where he found Primeau and five tents of First Nations people—likely Cree—who had already traded most of their best furs to Franceways. Cocking was upset to find that they had traded about 100 beaver for 16 litres of liquor along with coats and hats for two leaders. "I endeavoured all in my power to prevent the Natives giving away their furs, but in vain," he wrote.

Around this time, Cocking made two journal entries

that show his complete lack of understanding of both Canadians and First Nations people. On May 22, he wrote that twice he had been invited to Franceways' house to eat with him and was not impressed with his behaviour. "He is an ignorant Frenchman. I do not think he keeps a proper distance from his men; they coming into his apartment and talking with him as one of themselves." Then a few days later, "It surprises me what a warm side the Natives hath to the French Canadians."

On May 27, Cocking met Franceways and Primeau again at The Pas, near today's boundary between Saskatchewan and Manitoba. Franceways told Cocking that he had already sent two large canoes of furs to Grand Portage on Lake Superior and was planning to leave in a few days with a third loaded canoe. Cocking was undoubtedly envious of Franceways' success, but he was positively indignant when Primeau told him that he was going along with Franceways to Grand Portage to see his friends. Cocking scolded Primeau, telling him "that he was doing wrong [to leave] as he was under a written contract to serve the Company."

Cocking arrived back at York Factory on June 18, 1873, after being away for almost a year. Factor Graham was not impressed with the results of his trip.

Andrew Graham
During his 26 years with the HBC, Andrew Graham wrote extensively about company trading methods. Originally, he

had opposed both the establishment of inland posts and the sending of HBC servants inland. In 1768, he wrote that for the past 14 years "servants have been sent yearly inland to promote the fur trade, by making presents and inviting down strange Indians, but have increased the trade at York Fort nothing worth notice." He went on to say that he did not see how trade could be increased in this way, the servants "being ignorant poor labouring men of no abilities, who like to go for no other reason but to lead an idle and vagrant life amongst the natives." Graham also believed that servants were unsuitable to be sent inland because Native people looked on them as slaves, while they considered factors and officers to be great men. "This proceeds from their seeing the first set of men turned out to daily labour, while the other set walk about ordering and directing."

Graham also disagreed with critics who said that the HBC would get more pelts if people were paid more for them. He argued that if they were paid more per pelt they would catch fewer. He gave as an example a man bringing down the equivalent of 100 made beaver to York Factory and trading 70 of them "for real necessaries." When it was suggested to this man that he trade for more items that Graham considered necessities, his response was, "I have traded sufficient to serve me and my family until I see you again next summer." The man then drank one half of his remaining beaver and traded the other half "for baubles," Graham wrote disapprovingly.

However, by 1772, when he sent Cocking on his inland trip, Graham had changed his mind regarding inland posts. He sent a memorandum to the HBC London Committee arguing that a permanent inland post should be built.

Graham wrote a detailed description of life at York Factory during his time there. He said that the fort was well built of logs, with a double row of strong palisades, and had a "good class of quarters." On the riverbank near the fort was a half-moon-shaped battery with 15 cannons. Three kilometres below the fort was a second battery of 10 cannons and a powder magazine. Although these two batteries commanded the river, Graham said that the shoals and sandbanks across the mouth defended the factory better than the cannons because they kept ships eight kilometres away from the fort. York Factory, which shipped anywhere from 7,000 to 33,000 made beaver each year, had a very large staff, led by the chief factor. He was assisted by the second factor, the surgeon, sloop and brig masters, and the captain of the HBC ship when he was in port. Below these men were the skilled workers—accountant, writer, trader, steward, armourer, shipwright, carpenter, cooper, blacksmith, mason and tailor—and finally the servants or labourers. The men worked from 6 AM to 6 PM in summer and from 8 AM to 4 PM in winter.

Graham retired in 1775 and returned to Scotland.

Samuel Hearne

Hearne, who was born in London, enlisted in the Royal Navy when he was only 12 years old and saw considerable action during the Seven Years War. In 1766, he joined the HBC. He was chosen to head a northern expedition looking for a northwest passage and rumoured copper deposits. He was forced to abort his first two expeditions when his travelling companions stole all his food and other belongings. During the second expedition, he was abandoned to wander alone without food or shelter for three days before he was rescued by a Cree-Chipewyan leader named Matonabee. He was finally successful on his third attempt, beginning in December 1770, because Matonabee guided him. Hearne took few trade goods with him. Matonabee, on the other hand, had purchased gunpowder, shot and tobacco from the HBC before leaving and traded them "with a liberal hand" for furs during the trip.

When they reached the Coppermine River in July 1771, Hearne became the first European to reach the Arctic Ocean overland. To his great disappointment, he saw no signs of a northwest passage and found only one chunk of copper of any significant value. Hearne finally arrived back at Fort Prince of Wales (also called Fort Churchill), located on Hudson Bay at the mouth of the Churchill River, on June 30, 1772, after 19 months of travel. He wrote in his journal:

> Though my discoveries are not likely to prove of any
> material advantage to [either] the nation at large or . . . to
> the Hudson's Bay Company, yet I have the pleasure to think
> that I have fully complied with the orders of my masters
> and that it has put a final end to all disputes concerning a
> northwest passage though Hudson's Bay.

In 1773, Hearne was chosen to found the first HBC inland post. He selected a site strategically located near the Saskatchewan River about 100 kilometres west of The Pas, which he named Cumberland House. The first winter was difficult for Hearne, who had to work with inexperienced Orkney servants instead of the skilled First Nations people with whom he had made his Coppermine trip, but he emerged as an excellent leader. In spring, he proudly led a flotilla of 32 canoes of furs to York Factory. He only spent one year at Cumberland House, as he received a promotion to command Fort Prince of Wales in 1775.

After all the difficult years, Hearne was finally able to enjoy life at Fort Prince of Wales. He married and turned his residence into a miniature zoo. He had several beavers that were so domesticated that "they answered to their names and followed as a dog would do." They liked to be petted and were so fond of the women of the fort that if the women were away for any length of time, on their return the beavers crawled onto their laps and behaved to them "like children who see their parents but seldom."

This engraving of Fort Prince of Wales is based on a 1797 drawing by Samuel Hearne. PROVINCIAL ARCHIVES OF MANITOBA/HBC ARCHIVES N3115

Hearne's relatively idyllic life came to an end when the French attacked the fort in August 1782. The fort journal entry for August 8 stated that eight canoes of Cree were there ready to trade that morning, while a band of "northern Indians" (Dene or Chipewyan) had recently left. When a sail was spotted in the afternoon, the residents assumed it was the expected fall supply ship. When two other sails came into view, however, they immediately concluded that they were enemy ships from France. An almost global naval war between France, who supported the Americans, and Britain had been going on since the beginning of the American War of Independence.

French longboats landed the next morning, just out of range of the fort's cannons, and a lone man accompanied by a drummer walked to the gate. Although the fort was built to withstand an armed attack, Hearne only had 38 men and realized that the French would quickly defeat them. As a result, to the shock of the attackers, Hearne threw open the gate and ran a white tablecloth up the flagpole as a flag of surrender. The French imprisoned the HBC men on board the French ships, then stripped the fort of valuables and destroyed it.

Although the French commander left a stockpile of food for the Homeguard Cree, it was not enough for the winter. As a result, the Cree set off to walk the 240 kilometres to York Factory. Hearne would return to Hudson Bay the following year and re-establish Fort Prince of Wales, but his wife perished during the difficult winter while he was gone.

Matonabee
Matonabee was a handsome six-footer, who had been born in Fort Prince of Wales to a Cree slave woman and a Chipewyan hunter. Adopted by an HBC employee, Matonabee was probably the only Chipewyan of his time who was at home both inside an HBC fort and out on the Barren Lands, the treeless, sparsely populated area lying between Hudson Bay and Great Bear and Great Slave lakes. He was so skilful at maintaining the uneasy peace between various northern First Nations groups that he was acknowledged as chief over all of them. Samuel Hearne described him with great respect:

[He had] a scrupulous adherence to truth and honesty that would have done honour to the most enlightened and devout Christian [and a personality that was a mixture of] the vivacity of a Frenchman and the sincerity of an Englishman with the gravity and nobleness of a Turk.

In 1775, Matonabee arrived at Fort Prince of Wales with 300 Chipewyans and the largest number of pelts ever delivered to the HBC by Chipewyans. He naturally expected many gifts for himself in addition to the trade goods owed for the pelts. Hearne was exceedingly generous. The gifts included a captain's uniform for Matonabee and complete outfits for his six wives, eight guns, 65 kilograms of gunpowder (with shot, ball and flint), many hatchets and other tools, plus a great quantity of tobacco and blankets. Despite Hearne's generosity, Matonabee was not satisfied and bargained for even more. When Hearne objected, Matonabee replied that he would carry his goods in future to the Canadian traders, where he would get his own price for them. That even a friend of the HBC would threaten to switch loyalties indicated how vulnerable the HBC had become. As a result, Hearne gave in to Matonabee's demands, giving him goods to the value of 1,100 made beaver.

Despite Matonabee's early success, his life ended in tragedy. His prestige and authority were so closely tied to the English and the HBC that he hung himself shortly after the French took over York Factory in 1782. As a result of his death, his wives and four of his children starved to death the following winter.

Michilimackinac Traders Go to Saskatchewan Country

Alexander Henry the Elder continued to trade in the Great Lakes area until 1775, when he and Cadotte left Sault Ste. Marie for the Saskatchewan River country. By the time they arrived at The Pas in September, they were part of a fleet of 30 canoes and 130 men, including Peter Pond.

The Pas was a village of 30 families led by Chief Chatique (The Pelican), described by Henry as a corpulent man, over six feet tall "of a very doubtful physiognomy." In other words, his face was not handsome, and his expression was neither kindly nor welcoming. Chatique invited the traders into his tent. Although they suspected him of evil designs, they knew they must not show fear and thus accepted his invitation. Once inside, they immediately found themselves surrounded by armed men. Chatique told them that because he had the power to prevent them from going farther, he expected them to be "exceedingly liberal" in their presents. Then he listed exactly what gifts he expected: three casks of gunpowder, four bags of shot and ball, two bales of tobacco, three kegs of rum, three guns and some smaller items. His demands should be considered quite reasonable, he said, since he had enough men to take all of the traders' property without their consent.

The traders had no choice but to comply. Afterwards,

they hastened away, hoping that they had seen the last of Chatique. Almost immediately, however, they saw a canoe racing after them. It was Chatique. He boarded one of the traders' canoes, spear in hand, and demanded another keg of rum. The traders were tempted to kill him but decided that would be unwise. After they yielded to his new demand, he left as quickly as he had come, and that was the last they saw of him.

Henry had a much friendlier welcome when he visited the village of an Assiniboine chief called The Great Road on the western plains a few months later. About a day's journey from the village, two messengers arrived to formally welcome Henry and his companions and to accompany them to the village, where they were met by an armed guard who conducted them to the lodge assigned to them. Several women waited upon them in the tent, making the fire and bringing them water for washing.

Soon they heard a town crier inviting the townsmen to a feast in The Great Road's lodge and warning them that if they didn't behave "with decorum" toward the strangers, they would be punished. A man who appeared to be a lesser chief entered their tent and invited them to accompany him to the feast. On their arrival at The Great Road's lodge, he rose to greet them and thanked Henry for travelling so far to visit him. They sat on bearskins and took part in the usual pipe ceremony. The pipe, with a bowl of red pipestone and a four-foot (1.2-metre) stem, was passed around by an attendant. Then the chief made a lengthy speech, after which everyone present began to cry. Henry had previously been told that this was in honour of their deceased relatives; otherwise he would have concluded that a terrible calamity had just occurred. After about 10 minutes, everyone dried their eyes, and each guest received a plate of boiled buffalo tongue. Once they had eaten, The Great Road dismissed the guests by shaking hands.

Henry described The Great Road as being a tall man with a darker than average complexion, whose appearance "was greatly injured by the condition of his head of hair." Henry was told that each person had an object that was sacred to him. It was usually an animal, but in the case of The Great Road, it was his hair. Henry was assured that The Great Road's hair had never been cut or combed since his childhood. It was, however, in the care of a spirit who dressed it while he slept. "All this might be," Henry wrote, "but the spirit's style of hair dressing was at least peculiar; the hair being suffered to remain very much as if it received no dressing at all, and matted into ropes, which spread themselves in all directions."

The same evening, Henry and his men were invited to a second feast; this time, women were included among the guests. The next morning, they arose at daybreak and toured the village, which consisted of about 200 tents, each housing from two to four families. Four soldiers attended them, but this was insufficient to keep off the women and children, "who crowded round us with insatiable curiosity." They were also accompanied by numerous dogs, "all howling frightfully."

In mid-morning, Henry returned to his tent and met with The Great Road and nearly 50 other men. The Great Road told him that he wanted to bring his whole village to visit the white man's fort. After his speech, The Great Road and Henry exchanged gifts. The chief presented Henry with 20 pelts each of beaver and wolf, while Henry gave the chief one kilogram of vermilion and a few fathoms (one fathom measures 1.8 metres) of tobacco. The two men also agreed to depart for Fort des Prairies after five days. As Henry put it, when the chief left his tent, "I believe that we were reciprocally pleased with each other."

After living an adventurous wilderness life until he was 57, Henry finally settled in Montreal as a merchant. Prominent in both business and social circles in Montreal, he lived to the age of 85.

3

Two Fur-Trade Families

*Please make my excuse to Madam Chaboillez ... let her know
I will execute her orders for the additional quantity of corn she
has ordered. The rum I cannot promise until I have fulfilled
my engagements. Let her know also that her canoes was [sic]
the first men here this spring and took ... [almost] everything
that Monsieur Chaboillez was to get.*

—LETTER FROM JOHN ASKIN, JUNE 6, 1778

The Chaboillez Family

Marguerite Larchevêque Chaboillez was a 29-year-old wife
and mother of five young children in 1778. She also acted
as Montreal agent for the family's fur-trade business while
her husband, Charles Jean-Baptiste Chaboillez III, was

away in le pays d'en haut ("the high country," which was the name given to the territory north and west of Quebec by the Canadians). Letters written by Michilimackinac merchant John Askin, who supplied many well-known fur traders with trade goods and provisions, make it clear that Madame Chaboillez was an integral part of the business, not a mere figurehead.

A week after his June 6 letter, Askin wrote directly to Madame Chaboillez to tell her that he had delivered the goods to her clerk, who had left to meet her husband at Grand Portage. He closed by saying, "It will be my pleasure to serve you at all times as occasion may present, and you may be assured that I shall always keep an eye on your interests."

The Canadian branch of the Chaboillez family was descended from Charles Chaboillez I, who was born in France. His son Charles Chaboillez II was born in Montreal and died at Michilimackinac. He was a trader who had a post on St. Joseph Island. He married Marie-Anne Chevalier of Michilimackinac, whose parents had moved there from Montreal in 1718 and become leading merchants. Madame Chevalier, Marie-Anne's mother, tended the business while her husband was away on trading trips, and she continued the business after his death. Following her marriage to Charles Chaboillez II, Marie-Anne probably worked in the family fur-trade business, just as her mother had done. Marie-Anne moved to Montreal after her husband's death in 1757. We know she continued the business there because there is a record of her son, also named Charles, sending pelts to his mother and brother in Montreal in 1765.

Charles Jean-Baptiste Chaboillez III was born and died at Michilimackinac. He married Marguerite Larchevêque, daughter of a wealthy Montreal trader, in 1769. When they married, the couple had a combined fortune of 70,000 livres. Their daughter Marie-Marguerite married Simon McTavish, head of the NWC, and their eldest son, also named Charles, became a partner in the NWC.

About 1780, Charles Chaboillez III began spending winters in Montreal and summers on trading trips. His wife acted as his agent in Montreal when he was away. After 1793, he spent less and less time in Montreal, and Madame Chaboillez received power of attorney over the business. By the time of Madame Chaboillez's death in 1798, the family had lost its earlier fortune and was deeply in debt; however it's not known what led to the financial difficulties.

Charles Chaboillez IV, son of Charles and Marguerite, became a clerk for the NWC in 1791 and kept a journal of his activities while he was in charge of the trading post at Pembina in 1797–98. He made frequent mention in his journal of what he called "pillaging" by the Ojibwa. In December, he wrote of giving one man a large keg of mixed rum because "he behaved very well and prevented the Indians from pillaging our people." At the same time, an HBC man was robbed of 10 litres of spirits, one new gun and a couple of blankets, and came very near to being killed.

Charles Jean-Baptiste Chaboillez (Charles
Chaboillez III) was a third-generation fur trader.
MCCORD MUSEUM M1588

On at least one occasion, Chaboillez did meet with violence. In late January 1798, a quarrel arose when a group
of Ojibwa traded for liquor with the Nor'Westers and at the
nearby HBC post. Someone killed four of Chaboillez's dogs.
When Chaboillez confronted this man, the latter attacked him
with a knife. Fortunately for Chaboillez, the knife only went
through his coat, and he seemed to make light of the event:

"I gave him a good beating which occasioned them [the Ojibwa] to be very quiet for the remainder of the night."

Chaboillez and Alexander Henry the Younger, nephew of Alexander Henry the Elder, who took over the post at Pembina in 1801, went south to Missouri country to trade with the Mandan twice. In 1806, on what was likely the last Missouri trading trip made by the NWC, they were accompanied by a young clerk named Charles McKenzie and a Mandan chief named Le Borgne (One-Eyed). The Mandan and Gros Ventres were quarrelling with the Cheyenne at this time, and Chaboillez and Henry feared the worst when the three groups met during their trip. The Mandan and Gros Ventres gathered on rising ground above the camp, and Le Borgne—who was on foot—asked Chaboillez to lend him his horse so that he could go to speak to the Cheyenne. Chaboillez did not relish lending his horse, which was "a famous runner," but reluctantly agreed to do so when Le Borgne "pressed him in a commanding voice."

The negotiations were successful. Le Borgne summarized the causes of their dispute with the Cheyenne and concluded, "I speak to you now not to reproach you or to praise myself, but to get your answer whether you prefer war to peace. Speak." The Cheyenne responded, "We did not invite you to our land to make war upon you . . . therefore, go home in peace."

Chaboillez and Henry decided that they should return north soon after the above confrontation. McKenzie would have preferred to continue trading in the Missouri country, but he was still an apprentice clerk who had to do what Chaboillez and Henry ordered. McKenzie completed his account of the trip by saying, "I was not a little proud when I considered that I was the first north trader who crossed the Missouri with four packs of beaver."

Almost all NWC partners were of Scottish or English birth. In 1799, when Charles Chaboillez IV became a NWC partner, he was likely only the second Canadian to have reached this position. His career apparently went well until after he was named proprietor of Fort Pic, located north of Lake Superior, in 1807. The report of the 1809 annual meeting at Fort William states:

Charges of a very serious nature having been brought against Mr. Chaboillez, respecting his transactions at the Pic last season, but the necessary proofs not being in readiness; it is fully understood that such evidence as the case may require, is to be produced next summer either to substantiate those charges, or to do them away.

It is unknown what the charges were because no further mention of them appears in later NWC minutes; however, Chaboillez retired from the NWC shortly afterwards at the age of 37. It appears that he was found guilty, but because his family was part of the fur-trade elite, he was allowed to resign rather than be prosecuted.

John Tanner and Net-no-kwa

The Chaboillez family was not unusual, as trading and trapping were commonly multi-generational family occupations at the time. Ottawa chief Net-no-kwa and her foster son John Tanner also worked together trapping furs. Tanner was a Kentucky farm boy who was captured by the Shawnee in 1789, when he was 9 or 10 years old. His Shawnee captors treated him very cruelly, but a couple of years later they met a woman named Net-no-kwa at Michilimackinac. Net-no-kwa, who was the principal chief of the Ottawa, had lost a son about John's age, and she proceeded to bargain for John as a replacement for her son. In his 1830 autobiography, John described her as a skilful negotiator, "perfectly acquainted with the dispositions of those with whom she had to negotiate."

Net-no-kwa's husband, Taw-ga-we-ninne, was an Ojibwa (Saulteaux) hunter from the Red River, who was 17 years younger than Net-no-kwa, according to John. Taw-ga-we-ninne "was of secondary importance in the family, as everything belonged to Net-no-kwa, and she had direction in all affairs of any moment," John wrote. Every spring, Net-no-kwa and Taw-ga-we-ninne went to Michilimackinac, where Net-no-kwa was highly regarded by the traders. She always carried a flag in her canoe and whenever she came to Michilimackinac, "she was saluted by a gun from the fort." The first time they took John with them, she was afraid that she would lose him if he were seen by the inhabitants of

Michilimackinac. As a result, she took him to the house of the trader Chaboillez, "with whom she had sufficient influence to secure [his] confinement for several days in the cellar."

John Tanner's hunting education began at about the age of 12. He saw other boys his age shooting pigeons, but he had never even discharged a gun up to that time. He asked his foster father, Taw-ga-we-ninne, if he could borrow his pistol and go hunting. Taw-ga-we-ninne loaded the pistol and handed it to him, saying, "Go, my son, and if you kill anything with this, you shall immediately have a gun and learn to hunt."

John found some pigeons close to camp, cocked the pistol and raised it to his face. Then he carefully brought the sight to bear on a pigeon and fired. The pistol flew out of his hand, but the pigeon was lying dead under the tree. He ran home in triumph, proudly carrying his pigeon. Only then did he realize that his face was "much bruised and covered with blood."

The second part of his education—learning how to trap—began the following winter when he was sent to make marten traps. Although he referred to them as traps, it is likely that they were actually snares, since he talks about making them, not setting them. The first day he made only three traps, while a good trapper would have made 25 or 30 during that time. He continued his attempts without success for some days until Taw-ga-we-ninne took him in hand and showed him what to do.

Before the end of John's first year with his new family, both his foster father and his older foster brother were dead due to accidents, leaving the family with no adult male to support them. Net-no-kwa left Grand Portage that spring for the Red River to hunt beaver, taking her remaining sons, Wa-me-gon-a-biew and John, with her. She had lent their canoe to a trader, who was using it to pick up packs of furs along the route to the Red River, so she asked other traders going that way to take her family with them to retrieve their canoe. When they caught up with Net-no-kwa's canoe, the men refused to return it. John described what happened next. "The old woman took it from them without their consent, put it in the water, and put our baggage on board. The Frenchmen dared not make any resistance. I have never met with another Indian, either man or woman, who had so much authority as Net-no-kwa."

Net-no-kwa, John and Wa-me-gon-a-biew travelled west as far as Portage la Prairie on the Assiniboine River. Here, John got another trapping lesson. The adults assigned a little creek to the boys and told them that they would be the only ones allowed to trap beaver there that winter. Net-no-kwa gave John three traps and showed him how to set them with the help of a string tied around the spring. John found beavers in two of his traps the next morning. Because he was not strong enough to remove the animals from the traps by himself, he had to carry the traps home one at a time on his back so his mother could help him.

In early winter, the men went out buffalo hunting, but they thought John was too young to go with them and laughed when they saw him put his gun in readiness. After the men left, Net-no-kwa led him to a stand of trees close to their lodge, "near which her sagacity taught her the herd would probably run." She was correct. The herd passed so close to John's hiding place that he was able to kill his first buffalo, a large cow, much to the satisfaction of Net-no-kwa. The older men returned home empty-handed.

After a couple of years, during which time John also killed his first bear, Net-no-kwa decided that they should return to Lake Huron. They had travelled as far east as Lac La Pluie when Wa-me-gon-a-biew announced that he was going to return to the Red River. When Net-no-kwa could not convince him to go any farther east, she gave up the idea of going herself. She wouldn't leave their 10 packs of 40 beaver pelts each with the traders, "not having sufficient confidence in their honesty." Instead, they cached the furs in a remote place in the woods and then travelled to Pembina, where Alexander Henry the Younger was in charge of the trading post. By spring, they had trapped 11 packs of beaver and 10 packs of other skins. They headed back to Lac La Pluie, where they found that someone had broken into their cache. Net-no-kwa was angry and "did not hesitate to ascribe the theft to the traders," but they never did find out who had taken their furs.

They took their remaining pelts to Grand Portage,

where the traders urged them to have their packs carried across the portage in wagons. Net-no-kwa refused, "knowing if they were once in the hands of the traders, it would be difficult, if not impossible, for her to get them again." When they reached the fort, the traders "treated her with much attention, and giving her some wine, induced her to place all her packs in a room, which they gave her to occupy." Then they tried "by friendly solicitation" to induce her to sell her furs. When that didn't work, they threatened her, and finally Mr. Chaboillez' son attempted to take them by force. Chaboillez (likely Charles Chaboillez IV) reproved his son, but Net-no-kwa still lost all the furs when she began to drink due to her disappointment in Wa-me-gon-a-biew's behaviour.

John was very upset. "Of all our large load of peltries, the produce of so many days of toil, of so many long and difficult journeys, one blanket and three kegs of rum only remained . . . I did not . . . witness the needless and wanton waste of our . . . property with that indifference which the Indians always seemed to feel." They returned to Lac La Pluie, where they had to get credit for 120 beaver skins in order to furnish themselves with winter necessities.

Although John was upset with Net-no-kwa for losing all their beaver pelts, he was very much attached to her and to the Native way of life. While he was courting a young woman, Net-no-kwa woke him early one morning and told him to get up and go hunting. "It will raise you more in the estimation of the woman you would marry, to see you bring home a load of meat early in the morning, than to see you dressed ever so gaily, standing about in the village," she told him. John got up and brought home a large load of moose meat after a successful hunt. Net-no-kwa was very pleased:

> It gave me no small pleasure to think that my conduct met her approbation. There are many of the Indians who throw away and neglect their old people; but though Net-no-kwa was now decrepit and infirm, I felt the strongest regard for her, and continued to do so while she lived.

John Tanner's later life was not happy. He made at least three unsuccessful marriages and was unable to restore close ties with his birth family when he finally made contact with them 28 years after his kidnapping. Finally, in 1846, he vanished at the same time as another man was murdered. Tanner, who had recently had a disagreement with the murdered man, was never seen again. Many people thought Tanner committed the murder, but there was evidence that another man could equally well have been guilty.

4

Pond and Tomison in the North-West

About nine o'clock on an early March evening the witness returned home from the house of his next-door neighbour Mr. Waden. About ten minutes or so later the witness heard two gun shots.

—JOSEPH FAGNIANT DE BERTHIER, TESTIFYING ABOUT THE MURDER OF JEAN-ÉTIENNE WADDENS

Murder at Lac la Ronge

When Joseph Fagniant de Berthier heard two shots that seemed to come from next door, he had just taken off his shoes, so he asked another man to go out to see what had happened. The latter returned almost immediately to report that Jean-Étienne Waddens had been shot in the leg. Fagniant rushed next door. As he was entering Wadden's house, he saw Peter Pond and his clerk leaving the house. Waddens, who was lying on the floor with his left leg shattered from knee to ankle, was yelling, "Get out of here you two, and I don't ever want to see you again." Then Waddens saw Fagniant. He said, "Oh my friend I am killed" and asked Fagniant to try to stop the bleeding and to get his first-aid salve. Fagniant found powder marks on Wadden's knee, and two or three bullets that had gone through his leg and were trapped in his pant leg. Having lost much blood, Waddens was now finding it difficult to talk, so he didn't answer when Fagniant asked him if Pond's clerk had shot him. Pond and Waddens had quarrelled about an hour before supper, so Fagniant had good reason to believe that either Pond or his clerk had shot Waddens.

Noted explorer and fur trader Alexander Mackenzie described Waddens as "a Swiss gentlemen of strict probity and known sobriety" and said that two men of more opposite characters than Waddens and Pond "could not perhaps have been found." Waddens had gone to trade at Lac la Ronge in northern Saskatchewan about 1779. The following year, a number of small trading groups decided to have Pond and Waddens represent them at La Ronge. Pond represented the larger of these small firms and Waddens the smaller ones. Not surprisingly, due to their very different characters, problems arose during their winter together. Mackenzie stated that on the day Waddens was shot, he had invited Pond and one of his clerks to dinner. In the course of the evening, Waddens was shot through the lower thigh. He then expired from loss of blood. Pond and the clerk were tried for this murder at Montreal and acquitted; "nevertheless their innocence was not so apparent as to extinguish the original suspicion."

Although there was an inquest into Waddens' death in Montreal, no record has been found of the trial Mackenzie says took place. It is possible that a formal trial did not occur because there was a question whether Montreal authorities had jurisdiction in the North-West, which at that time was under control of the HBC.

Pond in the North-West

Pond had first arrived in the Saskatchewan country in 1775, along with a group of other Michilimackinac traders, including Alexander Henry the Elder. In 1778, Pond was chosen to take four canoes representing the pooled interests of several Canadian traders into Athabasca country. He spent the winter of 1778–79 about 65 kilometres from Lake Athabasca, where he met many Chipewyans and Cree who had previously carried their furs to Churchill. They were glad to see traders coming to them to save them such a long journey. As a result, Pond procured twice as many furs as his canoes would carry. He cached the excess furs and returned for them the following season.

Pond explored waterways around Lake Athabasca and determined the approximate locations of Great Slave and Great Bear lakes from First Nations people in the area. In the winter of 1784–85, he drew his celebrated map that included the whole known area from Hudson Bay to the Rocky Mountains. From his conversations with First Nations people, he assumed that all the tributaries in the area gathered into a great river, now called the Mackenzie River, flowing to the northwest and into the Arctic Ocean. He also assumed a northwest passage.

Pond spent 1784–85 in Montreal and the United States. During that time, he testified regarding the death of Waddens and wrote to the lieutenant-governor in Quebec urging the British government to aid traders in establishing posts all the way to the Pacific. He also presented a copy of his map to the US Congress.

Alexander Mackenzie used Pond's 1785 map for his exploration of the Mackenzie River and found that it was correct; in fact, many people now believe that Mackenzie did not give Pond sufficient credit. Unfortunately for his later credibility, however, Pond became aware of Captain James Cook's exploration of what is now called Cook's Inlet in Alaska. As a result, when Pond redrew his map in 1787, he wrongly assumed that the Mackenzie River flowed west into Cook's Inlet instead of north to the Arctic Ocean. This map, together with another drawn in 1790, largely discredited Pond as an explorer and mapmaker.

On Pond's return to Athabasca from Montreal, he again came into conflict with other traders, including a man named

John Ross. Over the winter of 1786–87 competition between Ross and Pond became very serious, and in the spring news was received that Ross "had been shot in a scuffle with Mr. Pond's men." Although there was no indication that Pond was directly involved, this was the third instance of violence connected with him. Combined with his age of 48, it resulted in Pond leaving Athabasca country forever in 1788. In 1790, he retired to his Connecticut hometown and died in poverty in 1807.

William Tomison Establishes Fort Edmonton

William Tomison and Pond were almost the same age, both were fur traders and both had a reputation of being very difficult to get along with. However, the similarities ended there. Tomison, who had no formal education, was born in the Orkney Islands. His 50-year career with the HBC began in 1760, when he joined them as a servant. He became very successful and was at the peak of his influence and reputation in the late 1780s, when Pond's career was almost at an end. By this time, however, most of Tomison's colleagues found him increasingly disagreeable, and they grew to dislike him intensely over the next decade. The feelings were mutual. In June 1795, Tomison wrote to Joseph Colen at York Factory complaining about the "miserable set of men" left inland. According to Tomison, only two of the men "can fire a gun so that we are laughed at by the meanest Canadian that came from Canada."

Hudson's Bay Company employees at a portage on a trip from Lake Winnipeg to York Factory. GLENBOW ARCHIVES NA-1041-6

Tomison was sent inland to trade along the east shore of Lake Winnipeg in 1767 and south and west of Lake Manitoba in 1769. As a result of his reports from these trips, he came to the notice of the HBC's London Committee as a valuable man who knew the ways of the fur trade and was "greatly beloved by the Natives." In 1778, he was promoted to inland master and began to implement the new HBC policy of establishing posts close to those of the Canadian traders. Returns from inland posts increased greatly, and he was given almost universal praise by his superiors.

In October 1795, Tomison arrived at the NWC's Fort Augustus on the North Saskatchewan River. His task was to construct a rival trading house "a musket-shot away" from Fort Augustus. This post was given the name Fort Edmonton. Tomison's journal and letters written over the next eight months show a very hardworking and exacting man, a strict taskmaster who expected everyone to work as hard as he did. Within a week of their arrival, Tomison's men had felled and prepared sufficient trees to begin construction. In his journal entry for October 14, he wrote that he had "twelve men working at the building, four men getting stones for the chimneys, one man fetching meat, four men making a saw-pit, and the rest collecting small pine sticks for the roof."

Tomison compared his own outfit unfavourably to that of the NWC. He wrote that the NWC had 105 men and had received 18 canoes loaded with 450 pieces of goods, including 140 8-gallon (32-litre) kegs of high wine (160-proof West Indian rum). On the other hand, he only had 8 canoes manned by 32 men and loaded with 96 pieces of goods, including 33 kegs of brandy and a single keg of rum. To add

PEOPLE OF THE FUR TRADE

to the insult, Tomison weighed a roll of tobacco listed on the invoice at 75 pounds (35 kilograms) and found that it only weighed 54 pounds (25 kilograms).

He voiced another complaint when two young men arrived for tobacco, powder and brandy shortly afterwards. He could not provide brandy "without I had given the whole keg neat" because he did not have any small kegs. He said that his neighbours at Fort Augustus had two coopers at work daily making small kegs and that he had asked several years previously, without avail, that the HBC send him a cooper. "It must be a silly notion to send strong liquor inland without a cooper to make small kegs to divide it in. It is well known the natives have no kegs of their own," he wrote.

Tomison was critical of the quality of his trade goods as well as their quantity. On October 25, he wrote that "a young man that had a gun in credit two days ago came back with it today, as not fit to be used, being split two inches from the breech upwards." Tomison said that many people had suffered injuries or even lost parts of their hands when guns exploded. There were also complaints about ice chisels and axes that shattered in the cold.

Construction on Fort Edmonton proceeded so rapidly that Tomison had moved his goods into the house by the end of October, "notwithstanding it is not finished." On October 31, four men were sawing boards for partitions while the smith was putting parchment in the window openings. Two days later, three men laid the foundation for a "victual shed," apparently an ice house, while most of the remaining men "cut and floated down 200 sticks for stockading the front of the house." In mid-November, a crew covered the house with turfs, while another crew cut the poles for the stockade to their proper length. On November 23, they began construction of a building for the smith's forge, and a week later a crew hauled birch wood to make charcoal for the smith. Tomison recorded that on December 10, the smith and an assistant were making steels and awls, the tailor was making clothing for Native leaders, three men worked the saw pit, one man was ill and the remaining men were laying flooring.

The men continued to work very hard throughout the winter. The smith and the tailor both worked at their trades, some men hunted for meat and others cut and hauled firewood. Tomison and his assistants traded seven days a week, as he frequently mentions working on a Sunday. They apparently did not even celebrate New Year's Day, an important holiday for the Scots; his entry for January 1 merely reads, "Wind variable with clear sharp weather. It being the first day of the New Year did not put the men to duty."

At the end of April, Tomison planned to begin shipping furs to Hudson Bay, but low water in the river and prairie fires caused him difficulties. On May 2, 1796, he wrote that he had upward of 100 bundles of furs and only three canoes. "Without there is a rise of water it will not be possible for us to get down full loaded. I would have sent some by land but the ground is all burnt and there is no food for horses."

The following excerpt from a letter written by Tomison to Chief Factor Joseph Colen the following year shows the kind of behaviour that Tomison's colleagues found so objectionable:

> I find there is two pieces of goods left on account of carrying Thompson's things up, which I think must in the first place be a very great imposition on you and a much greater on the Honourable Company, for in my opinion that man that would have been a carrier for so base a man as Thompson ought to have both his ears cut off, which I should not have scrupled at had he been my brother . . . your most obedient humble servant, William Tomison.

The man Tomison referred to is David Thompson, who left the HBC when his contract expired and went to work for the NWC. Colen had little sympathy with Tomison's view. He noted in the margin of Tomison's letter that it was not known that Thompson had resigned from the HBC at the time his parcels had been sent. Also, Thompson himself had agreed that his parcels could be returned to England at his expense if the HBC thought carrying them inconsistent with their duty.

Tomison lived for his work. He never married, had no friends and only retired under protest. He spent his final years on the Orkney island of his birth and bequeathed most of his considerable estate to establish a free school for the local children.

CHAPTER

5

Traders and Trappers on the Saskatchewan

The French gentleman . . . was well-dressed, his behaviour easy, mild and polite. He understood English and [every sentence he spoke] was attended by a smile and a slight bow, our men grave and stiff as pokers. On leaving us he gave us his best smile and a low bow, in compliment to which our men nodded their heads, which was all they could do.
—DAVID THOMPSON ON THE DIFFERENCES BETWEEN
CANADIAN AND HBC TRADERS

The Rivalry Continues

David Thompson was sent to the Saskatchewan River country as a clerk to help establish South Branch House for the HBC in the summer of 1786. Born in London of Welsh parents,

Thompson had begun his seven-year apprenticeship with the HBC two years earlier when he was only 14 years old.

The HBC party built a log house 11 by 6 metres directly across the river from two small houses built by Canadian traders. The house was mudded and covered with earth. The roof and floor were made of split logs, and it had two chimneys constructed of mud mixed with chopped grass. It was divided into three rooms: a storage room, a hall for business and trading, and accommodations for the men, known as the guard room. Thompson, like Tomison at Fort Edmonton, soon found that the neighbours across the river had more trade goods and better quality liquor than the HBC.

A Scotsman named Thorburn headed one of the two posts across from South Branch. He was employed by McTavish and Company, which was actually the NWC, while the unnamed French-Canadian described above by Thompson was employed by a rival Montreal company. Although Thorburn was a Nor'Wester, like most of the HBC men, he strongly disapproved of Canadians in general. He told Thompson that some Canadians were of good character, "but it was too frequently otherwise." With little education and no books, they passed their time over the winter playing cards, gambling and dancing. To remedy this "sad state," Thorburn suggested that the merchants should unite to form only one company and "place at the head of each trading house men of British origin of sober and steady habits on whom they could rely."

Thompson Begins His Trading Career

The following spring, David Thompson went to Manchester House. From there, he set off as a member of a trading party of six. The HBC advanced goods to each man to the value of 60 to 80 skins at "about two-thirds of what the Indians pay." The goods Thompson received to begin his first trading expedition included 40 rounds of ammunition, two knives, six flints, a few awls and needles and about a kilogram of tobacco. For his personal use, he also received a bison robe, a blanket, some clothing and one horse, which meant that he had to walk the greatest part of the journey.

Thompson said that the trade between the HBC and the trappers was profitable to both parties, "but more so to the Indians than to us" because the furs "of no use to them" had to be shipped such a long way before they could be sold in London. He gave the example of a woman sewing leather clothing using a bone or thorn needle. Show her an awl or heavy needle, he wrote, "and she will gladly give the finest beaver or wolf skin to purchase it."

At Manchester House, Thompson's life changed forever. Had it not been for an accident when he was 18, he may have spent his entire career strictly as a fur trader. In December 1788, he badly fractured his right leg. While he was recovering and unable to work, he learned mathematics, surveying and astronomy from Philip Turnor, the official HBC surveyor. Thompson wrote that breaking his leg "by the mercy of God turned out to be the best thing that ever happened to me."

Attack on South Branch

Jacko Finlay, a Métis employee at the NWC's Upper Bow Fort on the South Saskatchewan River near Duck Lake, went out riding on a fine, late-June morning in 1794. As he reached the summit of a hill, he suddenly came within a few yards of some Gros Ventres coming from the opposite direction. They gave a war whoop when they saw him. He turned and rode at full speed back to the fort, pursued by about half a dozen horsemen, who fortunately stopped to steal a few horses picketed outside the fort instead of trying to follow him inside. Thus, Finlay had sufficient time to raise the alarm and bolt the gates. The Nor'Westers stationed themselves in the blockhouses, while the Gros Ventres advanced boldly up to the fort. At the first shots fired by the Nor'Westers, the Gros Ventres fell back behind a rise in the ground. From this protected position, they fired upon the fort for half an hour before their war chief advanced toward the fort gates. Finlay shot and killed him. The remaining warriors recovered their leader's body and retreated, threatening vengeance against the Nor'Westers.

Earlier that same morning, the Gros Ventres had attacked South Branch House, across the river from Upper Bow Fort. This was the fort that Thompson had helped construct in 1786. The outcome was much different there than at Upper Bow. Three men were out looking for horses when they saw the Gros Ventres coming. One of the men, a Cree, suspected that they were enemies and suggested returning to the fort. The others, mistaking the Gros Ventres for Assiniboines, ignored the warning and advanced to meet them. Only one man escaped, but accounts vary regarding how many people were killed or captured. At least three men were killed, and perhaps as many as eight or nine, along with the Assiniboine wife of the post manager and two of her children. Several other women were carried off as slaves.

The Gros Ventres, also known as the Rapid or the Fall Indians, lived between the North and South branches of the Saskatchewan River during the 18th century, but were gradually forced south by the Crees over the next century until most of them lived in Montana.

Duncan McGillivray at Fort George

Duncan McGillivray was a clerk working under NWC partner Angus Shaw and travelled with him to Fort George in the summer of 1794. McGillivray was nephew of Simon McTavish, head of the NWC. They did not find out about the attack on South Branch until they arrived at Cumberland House at the end of August. HBC factor William Tomison, on his way to Buckingham House near Fort George, had been waiting there for 10 days for the Nor'Westers to arrive so that the two groups could travel together. Everyone was very nervous during the trip from Cumberland House to Fort George. McGillivray wrote that scarcely a day passed "without producing appearances which are supposed to portend immediate danger . . . buffalo, a stag [and] a wolf have been successively mistaken for Gros Ventres." The traders only began to relax somewhat after they met some Assiniboines who told them that the Gros Ventres had escaped to the Rocky Mountains immediately after their attack on South Branch.

McGillivray described a typical trading session at Fort George. When a First Nations group arrived near the fort, the chief would send a few young men to announce their arrival and to receive the gifts that the traders normally gave on these occasions—some powder, a piece of tobacco and a little paint for their faces. When almost at the gate, these young men would salute the traders by firing off their guns in the air. The traders responded by hoisting a flag and firing a few guns. Only then would the chiefs and other leading men enter the fort, where they were disarmed and treated to a few drams of alcohol and a bit of tobacco. After smoking for some time, the men would relate the latest news, "relaxing from their usual taciturnity in proportion to the quantity of rum they have swallowed."

During this time, the women would set up camp outside the fort. Then the adults were given free drinks of rum for 24 hours or more before the actual trading began. The number of drinks depended on which First Nation the trappers belonged to and the prestige of their chiefs. The gens du large (wandering tribes) of the plains were treated less generously than were the Woodland Cree and Ojibwa because the commodities that the plains people could provide—chiefly horses, wolves, fat and pemmican—were less in demand than the beaver pelts of the woodland people.

This engraving of a buffalo pound is from an original 1820 work by Lieutenant George Back. LIBRARY AND ARCHIVES CANADA E10934544

In late November, some young men, likely Crees, arrived at Fort George from a nearby buffalo pound for supplies. The Nor'Westers sent them off with 8 litres of rum, one fathom of tobacco and some ammunition. McGillivray and 11 other men accompanied the hunters to observe how a buffalo hunt was conducted using a pound. On the first night, they slept in a thicket "under the open canopy of heaven," wrapped up in robes. Despite a very cold northerly wind and an eight-centimetre snowfall overnight, they "enjoyed a refreshing night's rest," McGillivray wrote.

They arrived at the pound at 10 o'clock the next morning. The chiefs welcomed them at the entrance of the camp, and the master of the pound conducted them to his lodge, where they were served a feast. After the feast, they watched the hunt take place. The pound consisted of a corral constructed on the downward slope of a small hill so that it was invisible until it was too late for the buffalo to avoid it. Two low fences began on either side of the entrance, gradually becoming farther apart as they extended away from the entrance to form a large V. The hunters waved their robes from behind the fences to direct the buffalo toward the entrance. Once the animals were inside the pound, they were killed with bows and arrows.

McGillivray and Gros Blanc

In November, some Blackfoot arrived in the area and sent several Cree chiefs as emissaries to Fort George with offers to return all the horses they had stolen from the traders the previous year. Their hope was that they would thus secure a friendly reception from the Nor'Westers and be allowed to trade at the fort. On the morning of November 26, about 70 or 80 Blackfoot appeared and marched slowly toward Fort George. Fourteen chiefs leading 14 horses advanced to the fort gate and delivered the horses to Angus Shaw, but he was not satisfied. He told McGillivray and several other men to choose 10 more horses from the Blackfoot camp. They did so, despite Blackfoot protests.

This was the same band of Blackfoot who had robbed McGillivray of his horse the previous year, and he was angry to learn that the individuals who had done so were not present. As a result, McGillivray entered the hall where the principal Blackfoot and the traders were meeting. There McGillivray sprang upon their greatest chief, Gros Blanc, in a rage and "offered him an indignity which he will always remember with anger and resentment." Gros Blanc had a reputation as the most daring and feared chief in the whole trading department, partly due to his immense size and partly due to his acts of personal courage. Gros Blanc threatened to retaliate with violence against McGillivray, but his relations persuaded him against it. McGillivray received a horse and some finely ornamented robes in compensation for his stolen horse. Following this incident, according to McGillivray, the Blackfoot no longer bargained so hard and accepted much worse deals than previously for their furs. Some of the Cree who were present "exulted much" in Gros Blanc's disgrace. One influential chief, whose brother had been killed by Gros Blanc, regretted that McGillivray did not kill him.

Chief Gros Blanc did not return to the fort the next spring, but he sent a long message saying that McGillivray had offered him an insult that "no man breathing ever did before." However, as a mark of his forgiveness, he proposed to adopt McGillivray as his little brother to replace his actual brother who had been killed in a war with the Snake Indians.

Alexander Henry the Younger met Gros Blanc about 15 years later in the fall of 1809. Henry was so taken by this "extraordinary corpulent man" that he asked for permission to measure him. Henry recorded that Gros Blanc was 5 feet 7 inches (170 centimetres) around his shoulders and 6 feet 4 inches (193 centimetres) around his loins. "He appears to be upwards of sixty years of age and generally rides on a white mule."

The Nor'Westers vs. the Independent Traders

The altercation with Gros Blanc was not the only one in which the hot-tempered Duncan McGillivray resorted to violence. In 1801, during the annual NWC meeting at Grand Portage, an independent trader from Montreal sent his clerk to trade nearby. McGillivray demanded that the clerk move his tents farther away from the portage and threatened him with violence. The clerk reluctantly agreed to move, but before he could do so McGillivray returned with men who slashed the clerk's tent with a dagger and threatened to cut his throat. They also cut up a tent that a NWC engagé had purchased and then made a bonfire of it as a warning to employees against purchasing goods from the competition. As a result, the clerk was forced to return to Montreal without selling most of his goods. The merchant who had employed the clerk sued McGillivray, who was sentenced by the Montreal court to pay damages of £500.

In 1806, the same Montreal merchant sent out clerks

with two canoes loaded with goods. At a point beyond Lake Superior, they were overtaken by Nor'Westers who felled trees across several portages, preventing them from travelling any farther. The men were forced to abandon their goods and retreat to Fort William, where they appealed to William McGillivray, Duncan's older brother, who had succeeded Simon McTavish as head of the NWC in 1804. McGillivray, at whose orders they had been stopped in the first place, refused to allow them to trade but did agree to pay for their goods at Montreal prices. As a result, the merchant lost money on the venture but thought it safer to accept McGillivray's payment rather than trust in obtaining justice in the courts.

A young clerk wrote that in 1802 two NWC men were suspected of boring gimlet holes in kegs of high wine belonging to some competitors. According to the clerk, such actions were called "witty tricks." In a more serious action, Duncan McGillivray unsuccessfully attempted to kidnap three former NWC men now working for the opposing XY Company, which had formed in 1798. McGillivray argued that a trade monopoly was good for British interests because it rendered First Nations people dependent on a single company for trade goods "and consequently industrious and subordinate." As a result, they would be faithful to the British and would "abandon the chase and take up the hatchet" if asked to in case of war.

Duncan McGillivray died of an unknown illness in 1808, when he was still under 40 years of age.

6

Traders and Homeguard in Northern Manitoba

Treat the natives with humanity and [justice] ... Keep an exact journal of your proceedings as well as expenditures, for your own justification and the Honourable Company's information. Endeavour to provide provisions in summer for your men's supply in winter and if possible engage a hunter for that purpose.

—HBC FACTOR JOSEPH COLEN'S INSTRUCTIONS TO
WILLIAM SINCLAIR IN 1794

The French Attack York Factory

William Sinclair first arrived at York Factory from the Orkney Islands on board the HBC sloop *Severn* in the summer of 1782, when he was about 16. In common with many young men, he was likely looking for adventure as much as a means of earning a living when he signed his first contract with the HBC. He certainly got more adventure than he had bargained for on his arrival at York Factory.

The HBC supply ship arrived on August 15, dropping anchor near the mouth of the Hayes River close to York Factory, where large ships unloaded cargo into smaller sloops. Almost a week later, three French sails were seen coming from the direction of Fort Prince of Wales. The supply ship's captain and the chief factor of York Factory decided that the ship should take on needed water and as many of the year's catch of furs as possible and immediately leave for England. The captain wrote in his log that they pulled up anchor and set sail about 9 PM, thinking it would be safer "to endeavour to pass the enemy ships in the night than . . . perhaps be gotten by their boats after they have taken the factory." The HBC supply ship sailed safely past the French warships.

The factor tried unsuccessfully to defend York Factory after the ship escaped. Fifteen HBC men drowned when the French ordered them onto longboats to be taken out to the French ships at anchor. The factor wrote:

> We had informed the French that the weather was too bad to proceed in sending the troops on board but they were determined. On this accident, however, a stop was put to any further embarkation. Preparation they are now making to blow up the magazine and burn the fort.

About 50 HBC servants were removed, leaving behind many wives and children. The French allowed about 30 HBC men to sail to the Orkney Islands aboard the sloop *Severn*—on which William Sinclair had so recently arrived—because the French did not have room for everyone on board their ships. As a result, Sinclair's first visit to North America was cut extremely short, although he did return the following year.

The French had also captured and destroyed Fort Prince of Wales, under the command of Samuel Hearne, in August of 1782. Immediately afterwards, the Homeguard Cree from Fort Prince of Wales set off for York Factory. When they arrived at York Factory, they were exhausted, hungry and ill. At least 17 people died during the trip. The raid also damaged the relationship between the Chipewyans and the HBC because the HBC's inability to trade for two seasons drove many Chipewyans to develop trade relationships with the NWC. According to HBC records, the French raid affected HBC finances so badly that the Company could pay no dividends for four years after, even though the French agreed to compensate the HBC for its losses after Great Britain and France signed a peace treaty in 1783.

William Sinclair and Nahoway

When Sinclair returned to York Factory in 1783, the factor trained him to be a steward. A steward in an HBC post was responsible for recording incoming and outgoing provisions and distributing them between the fort and the fall ship. During the rest of the year, he received meat from the Homeguard Cree hunters and preserved it for later use. Sinclair went to England in 1790 due to ill health. One year later, he wrote to Joseph Colen, asking to return to York Factory. Colen wrote to the London Committee, stating that Sinclair had "served your honours faithfully" for eight years before his ill health had obliged him to return home and that he "would be found very useful inland, as a writer. He is very active and understands the Indian language tolerably well."

Around 1792, William Sinclair married a woman named Nahoway (also known as Margaret). Little is known about her early life, but her father was almost certainly of English or Scottish origin, and she spent her youth at or near Fort Prince of Wales. As a child, she had made the difficult trip to York Factory after the French destroyed Fort Prince of Wales. Sinclair's only recorded mention of Nahoway is in his will. After listing bequests to his 10 sons and daughters, Sinclair continues, "To my beloved wife Nahoway, mother of all the aforementioned children, I leave the interest only of three hundred and fifty pounds [at] three per cent, for her use and benefit during the term of her natural life." Although Nahoway was under 45—and possibly as young as in her late thirties—at the time of Sinclair's death, she would have been considered elderly. In a society where women seldom had their names recorded and elderly widowed Native women were rarely treated with much respect,

Nahoway was an exception. After Sinclair's death, she was always referred to in HBC records as either the widow of Chief Factor Sinclair or by her name.

Although the York Factory journal does not mention Nahoway by name, it makes it clear that women played an important role in the work carried out at the factory. Because Sinclair and Nahoway were married for many years, and he spoke affectionately of her in his will, almost certainly Nahoway was a very accomplished fur-trade woman. Many mentions of women's work are made in the journal, including dressing moose and deer skins for shoes and plucking hundreds of geese to make pillows and feather comforters.

Many women were expert canoeists. When families were travelling together, the men normally paddled in the bow, looking out for birds or animals to hunt. Meanwhile, the women steered and held the canoe steady while the men were shooting. Because the HBC had few experienced canoemen in the early years of inland trade, women often paddled company canoes and were engaged as navigators. One trader wrote of meeting three small canoes loaded with provisions for a new inland post—each canoe crewed by a female steersman and one English servant. Factor Colen wrote that one of the main reasons for the declining number of canoes coming to York Factory in the 1790s was that the women were no longer allowed to accompany their husbands and help paddle the canoes. This "occasions much murmuring among the men and forces many to leave the service sooner than they wished to." Colen made no comment regarding a possible reason for this new policy.

William Sinclair as a Trader

William Sinclair began work as an inland trader for the HBC in March 1794 when he travelled from York Factory to Chatham House, south of modern Thompson, Manitoba, carrying a letter from Factor Joseph Colen to the trader at Chatham House. Colen wrote that Sinclair was "well adapted" to establish a new post, although he "perhaps may require instruction on the method of inland trade, you will please give him the necessary information." Sinclair established a post called Threepoint Lake House (officially York House), and soon after that he received the letter from Colen quoted at the beginning of this chapter.

Sinclair returned to York Factory from Threepoint Lake House four or five months later with four canoes and a few bundles of furs. He was there to meet the annual ship from England; however, it was delayed due to bad weather, and continuing bad weather after its arrival prevented the traders from returning inland with supplies even longer. They were delayed so long, in fact, that Colen outfitted two canoes with crucial supplies and appointed the best hands to carry them overland to prevent the inland servants from experiencing distress. Sinclair's outfit, which numbered seven men, was included in this group.

When Sinclair arrived at York Factory in June 1795,

he had 14 canoes of furs manned by 24 English and 20 Homeguard Cree employees. By early July, conflicts had broken out between the men, who had too much free time and access to alcohol as they waited for the fall ship to arrive from England. Colen complained in his journal report, "Self and officers busy employed in settling the men who are to return inland. This we find a very arduous task as the outrageous behaviour of most of your honour's inland servants is such that it requires all our exertions to bring them to a sense of their duty, which they have been ignorant of for many years, every man having been completely his own master."

When the fall ship arrived at the end of August, Sinclair signed a new three-year contract. Controversy had arisen over Sinclair's posting to Threepoint Lake House soon after he had arrived there the previous year. The manager of the Fort Churchill district argued that Threepoint Lake House was actually in his district and should be outfitted from Churchill rather than from York Factory. The Churchill manager accused Sinclair of deliberately trying to prevent Cree hunters from taking their furs to Churchill. As a result of these complaints, Colen wrote to the trader at Churchill in the fall of 1795, telling him that he had ordered Sinclair to relinquish Threepoint Lake House, even though Colen disagreed with the idea: "But how it's possible for Churchill to supply that place with goods to a much greater advantage to the Company than this settlement [York Factory] can is to me a mystery." Colen added that according to

David Thompson's chart and to one of the local hunters, Threepoint Lake House was actually two days closer to York Factory than it was to Churchill.

Colen instructed Sinclair to keep a watchful eye over the Canadian traders and erect a trading house nearby whenever he found a Canadian post:

> Those men you pitch on for this duty, if they are attentive, will be rewarded. You are to fix on a careful person to remain up next summer to take care of the goods etc. and whatever his resolves may be, let them send word down & I will communicate the same to the Honourable Committee. In short it is merit alone that will advance men in future in this service.

Joseph Colen

Joseph Colen, who was born in England, was hired as a writer by the HBC in 1785 to assist the factor and oversee the rebuilding of York Factory. He drew up plans for a new fort to be built on the foundation of the old one and began work immediately. In 1788, however, the Hayes River rose 10 metres and the new fort was severely damaged by flooding and ice. As a result, Colen began construction on higher land about two kilometres upriver from the original site.

William Tomison was named chief factor in 1786, but Colen took command of York Factory because Tomison was ordered to reside inland by the HBC London Committee.

Colen was still subject to orders from Tomison when the latter visited York Factory. Like others, Colen found Tomison difficult to get along with, and accused him of trying to thwart every one of Colen's plans that did not benefit posts on the Saskatchewan River.

Colen was very critical of rival traders:

> Two Canadian houses were erected in the centre of the [Homeguard] wintering ground . . . these Canadian traders are so awful, it is impossible to keep the few skins the Indians procure from them as they . . . collect the produce of the hunt almost immediately on animals being killed. This induced the [loyal] Indians to remove their tent to a great distance from these intruding traders . . . while others, who cannot refrain from liquor, employ their young men hunting to purchase a supply, by which many are kept almost in an eternal state of intoxication.

Colen sent several presents to the people in the wintering ground via the Homeguard Cree, who hunted to supply the HBC posts on the bay with food and offered protection in case of attack. He had intended to send Sinclair along with the Cree to collect and mark all their bundles of furs, but he changed his mind after consulting with one the men "who had much authority among them." The latter assured Colen that he "would pursue every step to preserve the furs equal to any Englishman."

In 1795, Colen was appointed as chief factor since

Tomison was supposed to retire; however, Tomison stayed on and built Fort Edmonton. Colen was recalled to London in 1798, and his salary terminated in March 1799. No reason was stated for what apparently was a forced retirement, but the committee was impatient with the rivalry between Colen and Tomison. Also, Colen was considered lax in overseeing accounts at York Factory and lacked knowledge of inland operations. He was "an innovator and a thinker, rather than a shrewd businessman," who had collected a personal library of some 1,400 books while at York Factory. He spent the remaining 20 years of his life in England.

Little is known of Colen's family life; however, according to the officer who replaced him, "Mr. Colen's girl . . . engaged a male companion who had long since been in the habits of her attention and affection" soon after Colen left for England. The officer went on to say that she and her children had "received every civility from me since Mr. Colen's departure . . . so no blame can be attached to me of her not residing near the factory should he again visit this country—which I know it was his wish when he went home."

7

Thompson Travels to the Pacific

The view now before us was an ascent of deep snow, in all appearance to the height of land between the Atlantic and Pacific Oceans. It was to me a most exhilarating sight, but to my uneducated men a dreadful sight . . . the scene of desolation before us was dreadful, and I knew it . . . Amidst various thoughts I fell asleep on my bed of snow.

—DAVID THOMPSON, JANUARY 10, 1811

Thompson Becomes a Nor'Wester

David Thompson, whose early career is described in chapter 5, is considered one of the greatest geographers and surveyors who ever worked in North America. His January 1811 ascent to the top of Athabasca Pass was the culmination of his many years of exploration. His musings on the event show him as a thoughtful, reflective man as well as a man of action. Thompson had a very powerful mind; Dr. John J. Bigsby, a physician and naturalist who worked with Thompson, stated that he possessed the ability to describe a scene "so clearly and palpably, that only shut your eyes and you hear the crack of the rifle or feel the snow flakes on your cheeks as he talks."

Thompson strongly opposed trading liquor to the Native people and never allowed any liquor in posts where he was in charge. He once did an end run around two partners who overruled his no-liquor policy. Thompson wrote, "I placed the two kegs of alcohol on a vicious horse, and by noon the kegs were empty and in pieces . . . I wrote to my partners what I had done; and that I would do the same to every keg of alcohol."

In 1795, Thompson received a letter from Factor Joseph Colen saying that he could not sanction Thompson making any further surveys, "however extensive the countries yet unknown." With his passion for exploration, Thompson could not accept this. Since his HBC contract was up for renewal, he decided to apply for a position with the NWC. He attended the annual NWC rendezvous at Grand Portage, where he was appointed as astronomer and surveyor.

In 1792, the 49th parallel from the northwest corner of Lake of the Woods to the eastern foot of the Rocky Mountains had become the proposed boundary between

British and American territories. The problem was that no one was certain where this parallel actually was; thus, Thompson's first task was to survey the 49th parallel and to determine the exact locations of all the nearby NWC posts. He left with a brigade of four canoes in August 1796 and spent two years doing this survey before returning to report to the NWC at their annual meeting.

Thompson was promoted to a partnership in the NWC in 1804 and two years later was sent to Rocky Mountain House to develop trade on the Pacific coast. The following spring he set off to cross the Rockies, accompanied by a small party that included his wife, Charlotte, and three young children. They travelled by canoe until the North Saskatchewan River became impassable, then they camped for 14 days waiting for the snow to melt on the height of land. During that time, they transferred the supplies and trade goods from canoes into "boxes of thin boards sewed together" in preparation for carrying the goods on pack horses. They resumed travel on June 25 and camped that evening at the summit of Howse Pass, 130 kilometres northwest of Banff. They struggled onward for five more days until they reached a large river flowing north. Because Captain Vancouver had written that the Columbia flowed south and west, Thompson didn't realize for several years that he had actually found the Columbia—commonly referred to as "the Great River of the West"—that day.

The party built birchbark canoes and transferred their

goods from the pack horses back into these canoes. They paddled against a stiff current until July 18, when the river widened into a lake. Nearby, Thompson built Kootenay (also spelled Kootanae) House, the first post on the Columbia River, where he spent the winter trading. The following spring, he continued his explorations into what are now northern Idaho and Montana. He promised the people— many of whom had never seen a white man before—that he would return later with more trade goods.

Thompson's Second Columbia River Expedition

After 1807, the NWC seemed to lose interest in the exploration of the Columbia, but their interest revived in 1810 when John Jacob Astor of the Pacific Fur Company established a base at the mouth of the Columbia. The NWC sent a memo to the British Foreign Office, expressing the company's regret that its earlier requests for government recognition had not been heeded and pointing out the urgency of government action now that Astor had gone to Oregon country. The memo suggested that a British ship should be dispatched to take formal possession of the shores of the Columbia.

The NWC not only petitioned the British government; they also instructed Thompson to proceed to the mouth of the Columbia. When Thompson tried to cross the Rockies via the Howse Pass, the route he had used on his first trip in 1807, he was stopped by some angry Peigans. They blamed their recent defeat at the hands of the Salish on the traders who had supplied the Salish with weapons and ammunition in return for furs. The Peigans pursued Thompson's party until snow began falling and covered their tracks. About an hour later, the Peigans came upon three grizzly bears that had smelled the tracks of Thompson's horses. According to Thompson, the bears "sat on their rumps and showed their formidable teeth and claws, which made the Indians return in haste; they were sure I had placed the bears there to guard the road I had taken."

As a result of this run-in, Thompson decided to go to the mouth of the Columbia via the previously unexplored Athabasca Pass. Excerpts from his journal describe some of the difficulties of travelling this route in winter:

December 30, 1810: Having made snow shoes and sleds . . . we commenced our journey to cross the mountains, and proceeded up the Athabasca River.

December 31, 1810: We proceeded but slowly and I had to reduce the weight of the loads of the dogs to less than two-thirds and make a log hoard to secure what we left.

January 10, 1811: As usual, the men up early, cooking a plentiful breakfast . . . to put themselves in a good condition for fasting, with which the passage of the mountains threatens them . . . We had to cut wood such as it was, and each took a little on his sled.

David Thompson is portrayed at work in this pen-and-ink drawing by C.W. Jefferys. LIBRARY AND ARCHIVES CANADA C-073573

It was also on January 10 that Thompson caught first sight of the height of land at the top of the Athabasca Pass. Because they had only been able to collect a small amount of wood, Thompson and his men were forced to spend most of the night out in the open without fire at the top of the pass. Early the next morning they started down, finding that both climate and vegetation quickly changed. Very soon they came to tall pine trees, as much as five to six metres around. The trees created what Thompson called a "most laughable vexatious business." The steep decline caused the sleds and dogs to speed up greatly. Soon, most of the dogs found themselves and their sleds tangled around large trees. As a result, the dogs received hard knocks against the trees. "Out of revenge they fought with each other, and we had to give them some raps on the head to bring them to their senses." Finally, they managed to untangle all of the dogs and sleds, and before sunset they had reached the bank of the Columbia River at the foot of the mountain.

Thompson had crossed the pass with eight Canadians, but five of them refused to go any farther and returned the way they had come. Thompson and the others dug a hole just over one metre deep and three metres square, which they lined with cedar to form a hut in which they spent the rest of the winter. They found the birchbark was too thin for canoes, so they constructed canoes of split cedar boards sewn together with pine roots.

The small group could not descend directly to the sea in the spring due to a shortage of men. On June 14, they arrived at Spokane House, where Jacko Finlay was clerk and 40 tents of Spokane people lived. Thompson was able to leave Finlay "a small assortment of goods to continue the trade." On July 3, Thompson, having hired sufficient men, set off on the last leg of his journey to the Pacific. After passing the junction of the Spokane River, Thompson set up camp and invited the chief men of the nearby village to come and smoke. Four pipes were lighted and "the smoking enjoyed as a feast." The chief made a long speech in a loud singing voice, asking that Thompson bring guns and ammunition, axes, knives and many other items to his village. The chief said they were able and willing to hunt and would be able to pay for everything they wanted. Finally, the chief asked permission for the women to come to see them. Smoking commenced again. "Each man took three hearty puffs as the calumets passed, but the women were allowed only one whiff, which they made a long whiff."

On July 9, 1811, at the junction of the Snake and Columbia Rivers, Thompson posted this notice: "Know hereby that this country is claimed by Great Britain . . . and that the North West Company of merchants from Canada . . . do hereby intend to erect a factory in this place for the commerce of the country around."

Finally, they came in sight of the Pacific on July 15, "which to me was a great pleasure, but my men seemed disappointed," Thompson wrote. It was three kilometres to Fort Astoria, trading post of the American John Jacob Astor, where two former Nor'Westers were in charge and "politely received" Thompson and his men.

During the winter of 1811–12 Thompson made several expeditions from Spokane House. That spring, Finlay and Thompson packed more than 4 tonnes of furs, which Thompson transported east via the Athabasca Pass bound for Montreal. It would be the last time Thompson crossed the Rocky Mountains.

A Successful Marriage

Scotsman Patrick Small was a NWC wintering partner at Île-à-la-Crosse and the father of two daughters who married well-known fur traders. Nancy became the wife of John McDonald of Garth, and Charlotte married David Thompson in 1799, when she was 13. While some writers have fictionalized a romantic meeting and love at first sight for the couple, no one knows what actually happened because Thompson wrote little about his personal life. His journal entry about the marriage was brief: "This day married Charlotte Small." Later, discussing trade with the Cree, he wrote, "My lovely wife is of the blood of these people, speaking their language, and well educated in the English language, which gives me great advantage."

Two of Thompson's rare journal references to his children occur in June 1808. On June 19, he wrote, "One of my horses nearly crushing my children to death from his load being badly put on, which I mistook for being vicious; I shot him on the spot and rescued my little ones." The next day, his two-year-old daughter, Emma, went missing while they were travelling by canoe. He reported that after searching most of the morning, they found Emma sleeping under a bush.

A few snippets of letters Thompson wrote to his wife also remain. In December 1810, he wrote to her at Pembina:

> My dear Charlotte, In a few days I will be sending six or seven of my men to Rocky Mountain House to get pemmican and

other supplies and they will carry this and my other letters with them. I am hoping they will return with a letter from you, for I am anxious to know how you are faring . . . I wonder if this will reach you by Christmas? I wish you and the children every blessing; I long for news of you. As ever, David.

In 1812, Thompson retired after 28 years in the wilderness and moved his family to Canada. Charlotte lived as the wife of a wealthy landowner until economic disaster struck with the collapse of the NWC. A grandson described her as "slightly built, active and wiry, with a coppery complexion. She dressed plainly but neatly, loved her home and was an excellent housekeeper . . . she was extremely reserved except when among family."

David and Charlotte Thompson died three months apart in 1857, after 58 years of marriage. In most cases when a fur-trade marriage lasted until death, the husband remained in the North-West with his family upon retirement. It was much more common for the husband—like Charlotte's father Patrick Small—to abandon his family and return to the country of his birth or to move to Canada. Despite the few details we have about the Thompson marriage, it is fair to describe it as one of the great love stories in Canadian history.

8

Settlers vs. Traders

Sometimes armed parties boarded the Hudson's Bay boats . . .
at other times they plundered and burnt the trading houses of
that Company, wounding and otherwise ill-treating the ser-
vants who rose in defence of their master's property . . . the
perpetrators themselves . . . boasted of these violent acts as
meritorious services to the NWC.

—NWC CLERK JOHN PRITCHARD

John Pritchard and the Pemmican Proclamation

In 1801, John Pritchard arrived from England and signed up
for a five-year term as a clerk with the XY (New North West
Company). Although he became a Nor'Wester after the two
companies rejoined in 1804, he was often critical of NWC

actions against the HBC and First Nations people who dealt with the HBC.

In 1812, Pritchard received a letter from a NWC partner asking his opinion of Lord Selkirk's colony. The partner said that he was confident that the colony could not succeed if the NWC clerks at the Red River "all did our duty, of which he did not entertain the smallest doubt."

Pritchard replied that he considered it his duty, "as a faithful servant of the NWC to oppose the settlement by every fair means in my power." In the winter of 1813–14, Pritchard was ordered to buy up as many provisions as he possibly could. "I did so, giving an advanced price, by which means I procured one-third more than the quantity usually required for the use of the NWC." In the spring, he brought these provisions to the Souris River Post from the Qu'Appelle River. When he arrived at Souris, he learned about the infamous "Pemmican Proclamation" issued by Captain Miles Macdonnell, governor of the Red River Settlement, on January 8, 1814.

The Pemmican Proclamation stated that the welfare of the settlers made it essential to provide enough food for their support. Thus, for a period of one year, no one trading in furs or provisions within the territory should take any provisions out of the territory except for those necessary to carry the trading parties presently within the territory "to their respective destinations." Macdonnell added insult to injury—in the eyes of the Nor'Westers—by saying that the traders were required to apply to him "to obtain licence for the same" in order to remove these necessary provisions from Selkirk's territory. The proclamation concluded by saying that the provisions thus procured would be paid for "by British bills at the customary rates."

Not surprisingly, the Nor'Westers let it be known that they had no intention of obeying the proclamation. They sent letters to all their trading posts, calling their people to a meeting at Fort Gibraltar, the NWC fort near the Red River Settlement, and began buying up all available pemmican supplies to keep them from Macdonnell. Pritchard was ordered to remain at Souris with the provisions he had brought from the Qu'Appelle River until he received further orders. Shortly afterwards, Sheriff John Spencer arrived at Souris from the Red River with Macdonnell's warrant to seize the provisions. When the Nor'Westers refused to open the fort to Spencer, he ordered his men to force open the storehouse with hatchets. They did so and seized 600 sacks of pemmican, which they transported to Brandon House, the nearby HBC post.

Macdonnell was apparently unconcerned about the NWC reaction to his proclamation. He wrote to HBC factor William Auld, "I have sufficient force to crush all the Nor'Westers in this river should they be so hard as to resist openly my authority . . . We are so well armed and I have a parcel of fine active stout fellows that will execute any order they receive."

Auld had strongly opposed the creation of the Red River Settlement and wrote of Macdonnell, "If Lord Selkirk had advertised for a fool of the first magnitude he never could have better succeeded than he has done with the present man." However, despite his reservations about Macdonnell, Auld acknowledged the governor's jurisdiction and supported the principal that provisions should not be taken from the territory without a licence from Macdonnell.

Pritchard left for Fort Gibraltar after the attack on Souris. When he arrived, he learned that an agreement had been made between Macdonnell and a group of NWC partners, led by John McDonald of Garth, who had arrived opportunely at the moment when the other partners were going to make an attack upon Macdonnell. Pritchard was asked to write "some papers of a conciliatory nature . . . under the direction of the partners present." The agreement was signed by Macdonnell and all but one of the Nor'Westers.

The Nor'Westers then went to the 1814 rendezvous at Fort William. Pritchard wrote that William McGillivray "was exceedingly angry with his partners" for making an agreement with Macdonnell. When Pritchard observed that a different conduct would have led to bloodshed, McGillivray "replied with a sneer" that he knew better and that it was not the value of the provisions he regretted, "but the insult offered to the concern."

Although the agreement was officially endorsed at the annual NWC meeting, those Nor'Westers who had permitted John Spencer and the HBC to seize pemmican under their control were censured at a special meeting and "a full determination was taken to defend the property at all hazards."

Pritchard Becomes a Settler

By the 1814 rendezvous, Pritchard had decided to resign from the NWC and become a settler at the Red River. He offered to buy goods from the NWC to the value of the money they owed him for his work if they would give him passage back to the Red River. He also would bind himself to a penalty of £1,000 "never to oppose the interest of the company in the capacity of an Indian trader." McGillivray refused, saying that he "could not countenance" Pritchard settling at the Red River after what had happened. He offered Pritchard some land at York instead. A fellow clerk advised Pritchard not to return to the Red River contrary to the wishes of the NWC or they would get him murdered on the road.

As a result of this warning, Pritchard went to Montreal instead, but while he was there he got further evidence that the NWC was "determined upon the ruin of the colony at Red River." Pritchard decided that he must return to the settlement immediately to warn Governor Macdonnell. He travelled via Hudson Bay, walking most of the way on snowshoes and pulling a sledge with provisions. He left Montreal at the end of October 1814 and arrived at the Red River on April 15, 1815. His journey was in vain, however, as Macdonnell was arrested the day after Pritchard's arrival and taken east by the Nor'Westers under guard soon after. Pritchard tried to farm, but conditions went from bad to worse. In his words:

> The day on which the governor was carried off, the firing upon our houses was renewed with unabated fury. Thus, deprived of our chief magistrate, our servants inveigled away, abandoned by many of our brother settlers, assailed by a lawless banditti bent on our destruction, our cattle destroyed, and our fields laid waste, we were compelled to quit the country.

The settlers arrived at Jack River House, an HBC trading post on Lake Winnipeg, in early July. HBC employee Colin Robertson, whom Pritchard had met in Montreal, caught up to them there and agreed to conduct them back to the colony. By the time that Robert Semple arrived in November as the new governor of the colony, Robertson had the colony up and running again, and the winter of 1815–16 was quite prosperous.

Trouble broke out again the following spring, when a group of Métis led by Cuthbert Grant defeated settlers and HBC employees at the Battle of Seven Oaks on June 19, 1816. Governor Semple and 20 of his men were killed. Pritchard was taken as a prisoner to Fort William but was released shortly afterwards when Lord Selkirk arrived at Fort William. Selkirk sent him back to the Red River with a proclamation issued by the governor-in-chief of British North America, which Selkirk supposed would protect the settlement against further violence; however, Pritchard only got as far as Lac La Pluie before he was detained by some Nor'Westers who threatened that "if he proceeded, he would be assassinated." As a result, he returned to Montreal.

Cuthbert Grant

Cuthbert Grant, the son of a Métis woman and Scots-born wintering partner Cuthbert Grant Sr., was educated in Montreal following the death of his father. He returned to the North-West with the annual brigade in 1812 at the age of 19 and was posted to Fort Espérance on the Qu'Appelle River, under the command of John Pritchard.

Although many Métis were employed by the NWC, the community as a whole had not yet taken a strong position in the dispute between the Nor'Westers and the HBC. In order to gain Métis allegiance, the NWC named four men, including Cuthbert Grant, as "captains of the Métis" in the fall of 1814. Grant won over a considerable number of Métis and also actively worked to persuade settlers to accept the NWC's offer of transportation out of the Red River Settlement to Canada. In June 1815, Grant established a camp along the Red River six kilometres downstream from the colony to cover the departure of 42 colonists for Canada in NWC canoes. Grant's men began to harry the settlement and there were shots fired between the Métis and the remaining

Métis leader Cuthbert Grant was 19 years old at the time at the time this portrait was painted. LIBRARY AND ARCHIVES CANADA NLC008796

settlers. Finally, on June 25, Peter Fidler, who had been left in charge of the colony after the arrest of Governor Macdonnell, capitulated under an agreement signed by Grant as one of the "chiefs of the Half-breeds." No one signed the agreement for the NWC, making the Métis appear to be solely responsible.

Afterwards, Grant returned to the Qu'Appelle River and remained there until the following spring. In March 1816,

Grant was promoted to "Captain-General" of all the Métis, and in May he led a troop of 60 horsemen who ambushed boats bringing pemmican down the river. After capturing the pemmican, they escorted it down the Assiniboine River to be delivered to the fur brigades waiting on Lake Winnipeg. On June 18, they left Portage la Prairie. Grant led the Métis into the Battle of Seven Oaks the next day.

In October, Grant once again went back to the Qu'Appelle River, but he gave himself up in August 1817 after commissioner William Coltman arrived to inquire into the events at Seven Oaks and the whole dispute between the HBC and the NWC. Grant spent the winter of 1817–18 in jail in Montreal. In the spring, he was charged with the murder of several people, including Governor Semple, and with the theft of HBC property, but he jumped bail and fled to the North-West. Charges against him "were quietly shelved."

Not surprisingly, Grant was not employed by the newly merged HBC and NWC in 1821. Soon after, however, the head of the HBC concluded that Grant's exclusion from employment would only increase his prestige among the Métis. As a result, Grant received an appointment as a clerk and special constable in July 1823. This angered many of the settlers, and Grant retired from the HBC the following year after being assaulted by a group of settlers. He was granted land at White Horse Plains on the Assiniboine River west of the Red River Settlement, where he founded a Métis community and spent the remainder of his life.

9

Athabasca Country Traders

To behold the Northwest Company in all its state and grandeur, it was necessary to witness the annual gathering at . . . Fort William . . . [where] the leading partners from Montreal . . . ascended the rivers in great state, like sovereigns making a progress . . . Every partner who had charge of an interior post . . . felt like the chieftain of a Highland clan.

— WASHINGTON IRVING

Simon McGillivray and the 1815 Fort William Rendezvous

Although Simon McGillivray was in the family fur-trade business like his two older brothers, William and Duncan, he spent most of his career in London because of his lame foot. The agreement admitting Simon to the company stated that he was to "watch over its interests wherever they may come under his view, whether in Great Britain or in Canada." By 1814, he was the second-largest shareholder in the company, next to his brother William, who was head of the NWC. By this time, Duncan was no longer alive.

Simon attended the 1815 Fort William rendezvous in place of his brother William. It was his second trip to North America within a year, which suggests how serious the McGillivrays felt the NWC situation was at the time. Three major issues concerned them: many wintering partners seemed to favour coming to terms with John Jacob Astor, who had held control of the southwest fur trade since the end of the War of 1812; the HBC refused to give the NWC transportation access to Hudson Bay; and Selkirk's Red River Settlement.

Many of the wintering partners were very unhappy by the time of the 1815 rendezvous. No longer were they the proud Nor'Westers described by Washington Irving. They shared the McGillivray brothers' concern over events at the Red River Settlement; however, their other concerns were quite different than those of the McGillivrays. The wintering partners felt that they were forced to pay inflated prices for trade goods. They also believed that the value of their company shares was declining because they had to travel longer distances on extended trade routes while their trade territories were actually shrinking.

·   As a result, Simon found himself not only placating the winterers but also trying to block their desertion from the NWC itself. At least some of their hostility had been nurtured by enemies of the NWC, particularly Colin Robertson, who wrote to Selkirk shortly before the 1815 meeting that the NWC "is now ripe for a rebellion, their finances are at the lowest ebb, their promises to the young gentlemen are nearly exhausted."

The official minutes of the 1815 meeting no longer exist, but Simon kept a detailed account of the events. On July 17, he wrote that a very acrimonious discussion took place between the wintering partners and the agents, the latter including him and the Montreal-based partners. The topic was the exchange rate, which was the difference in value between British and Halifax currency. (Halifax currency was based on Spanish silver dollars introduced into British North America by merchants following the fall of New France in 1763.) The wintering partners thought the agents should absorb the whole loss of this difference, "that is to make us pay 20 or 25% for the honour of shipping their returns to England." Although all of the partners disavowed hostile feelings toward the NWC, Simon told them that their proposed measures—if not their motives—"were of a most hostile character." These measures "would certainly give great encouragement to the opposition" and might even go so far as to ruin the NWC. The wintering partners finally backed down.

The next day, an equally contentious issue arose. Wintering partner Dr. John McLoughlin refused to go to Athabasca and said he would retire if he was forced to do so. This was despite a unanimous vote posting him there. That vote was then rescinded "on the score of expediency," and he was ordered to Lac La Pluie. As a result, other partners then made threats in order to have their postings changed. Simon McGillivray concluded that "there are some secret but active enemies . . . at work in order to sow dissention [*sic*] and if possible destroy the concern."

Then, on July 22, the winterers complained that John McLoughlin was neglecting his medical work. "As usual," Simon wrote, "[they] blame the appointment, or in other words the agents." The annoyed McGillivray told the winterers "to settle the thing as they please." As a result, they decide to keep McLoughlin at Fort William.

The rendezvous ended on July 25. That day, the wintering partners sent Simon McGillivray "a complimentary letter" in which they appeared "rather ashamed of their conduct in the beginning." McGillivray sums matters up by saying that, despite the stormy beginning, the meeting "subsided into calm and we part very good friends."

Colin Robertson's Athabasca Plan

Colin Robertson was a flamboyant, red-headed, six-foot Scottish Highlander who had worked with the NWC from 1803 to 1809. He had originally submitted a plan to the

HBC in 1810, advising them to extend their operations to Athabasca country. It was rejected, but the revised proposal he submitted in 1814 was accepted.

"How it will end, God knows ... The time I am losing with this fleet may defeat the object of my voyage," wrote a frustrated Robertson on his trip from Liverpool to Montreal to implement his plan. This comment set the tone for the whole of his relationship with the HBC, which had officially begun in April 1814. The ship he was aboard had left Liverpool on May 22, but was delayed for three weeks at Cork while waiting for the convoy with which it was to cross the Atlantic. Almost immediately after the convoy set sail, it had to take shelter due to bad weather. Finally, in desperation, the commodore put out to sea on July 28 in a worse storm than that which had brought them to seek shelter in the first place.

The essence of Robertson's proposal was that the HBC should extend its operations into Athabasca country and that the Athabasca expedition must be manned by Canadian voyageurs led by former NWC officers. Robertson said that the HBC's Orkney-born servants "were only competent for the Bay-side posts and were thinking about retirement by the time they had learned to handle a canoe." Robertson proposed that he would go to Montreal, where he would recruit suitable officers from among the Nor'Westers and outfit the Athabasca expedition from an agency which the HBC would set up with him in charge. He didn't plan to actually go to Athabasca himself.

Colin Robertson, shown in this portrait made around 1821, was determined to expand HBC operations into Athabasca country.

LIBRARY AND ARCHIVES CANADA C-008984

John McDonald of Garth, who retired from the NWC late in 1814, wrote in his memoirs that he met Robertson in the village of Terrebonne near Montreal. According to McDonald, Robertson was headquartered in Terrebonne with about 400 voyageurs whom he was "fitting out for the Hudson's Bay territory." McDonald said that Robertson "became very troublesome, dangerous and insulting in the village, making it dangerous to any one connected with the NWC to pass the streets."

As a result, William McGillivray asked McDonald to try to evict Robertson's party from the inn they were using as headquarters, since the landlord's lease was about to expire. McDonald immediately left for the inn. As he walked up the steps, he was given a hard push which would have knocked him down, except that someone behind him held him up. McDonald had a cane containing a small sword in his hand. Pointing the steel point before him, he remounted the steps and rushed into the inn, which was crowded with voyageurs. McDonald told the landlord's wife, who was looking after the bar, that "the house must be clear" when he returned the next morning. Then he left with "all hands making a clear passage" for him, due to the sword in his hands. The next day, all was quiet at the inn, and two days later Robertson's group had left the village. However, there is no evidence that Robertson left because of McDonald's actions, and it seems most unlikely that Robertson would have recruited anywhere near 400 voyageurs.

Robertson's proposal to the HBC relied on five factors for its success: the NWC would not learn of his plans until it was too late for them to warn their wintering partners that the HBC was coming to Athabasca; Robertson would manage the Montreal agency outfitting the expedition; Robertson would be able to hire a suitable person to lead the Athabasca expedition; the Red River Settlement would provide provisions for the Athabasca traders; and the continuance of the War of 1812.

One of the selling points in Robertson's proposal had

to do with tobacco, which was vital to the fur trade with First Nations people. The most popular type of tobacco was North West Twist from Brazil. The NWC normally imported it from the United States, but John Jacob Astor of the Pacific Fur Company had cornered the market on North West Twist during the War of 1812 and refused to sell any to the Nor'Westers. He did, however, provide some to Robertson, who gleefully reported to his employers:

> I have got an excellent lot of tobacco for the Indian trade which belonged to Mr. Astor. The NWC have been obliged to purchase an inferior quality . . . as that gentleman held every ounce of North West Twist in the country. His enmity to the firm of McTavish, McGillivray & Co. is such that he has avoided dealings with them even where profit was certain.

Because Robertson arrived in Montreal so late in the season, he could not outfit an Athabasca expedition to leave until the following May, and the element of surprise was lost. In an attempt to hide his plans (and in agreement with Selkirk), Robertson planned to appear in Canada in the guise of a land agent sent out to negotiate the sale of townships on the Red River. Robertson met some disaffected Nor'Westers in Montreal and advised them to form a coalition of wintering partners against the McGillivrays. He also hired several former Nor'Westers (including John Pritchard and a former Pacific Fur Company employee named John Clarke) as officers. Robertson, however, did not feel that any of these men were suitable to lead the expedition to Athabasca. Of John Clarke he wrote, "He is not exactly the person that I wished at the head of the expedition, as his notions of general business are rather defective." As a result, he decided that he would have to spend at least one winter in Athabasca country rather than remaining in Montreal.

Another blow to Robertson's plan was that he could not outfit the expedition himself. He wrote in his diary that the Montreal business community was so much under NWC control that he had to hire an existing firm rather than form a new one that he could keep under his control.

The NWC had requested permission of the HBC to send a ship through Hudson Bay during the War of 1812, since their normal shipping route was closed due to the war. Robertson suggested to the HBC that, "You might offer to take out their furs in your ships, indeed allow them every indulgence but that of entering the Bay." This point, he believed was essential for destroying the NWC; however, when the War of 1812 ended in December 1814, the normal shipping routes reopened, thus rendering Hudson Bay less important to the NWC.

The Athabasca Expedition Launched

In May 1815, Robertson was finally ready to set off from Montreal for Athabasca country with a brigade of 16 canoes and 160 voyageurs, which he had outfitted by lavish expenditure of money and charm. Between Lake Superior and Lac la Pluie, Robertson met NWC canoes carrying Governor Miles Macdonnell and some settlers from the Red River Settlement east to Canada. Because failure of the colony would be a blow to Robertson's plan, he hurried on ahead of the rest of his brigade to see for himself what conditions were like at the Red River. Only four settlers remained there. About 50 others had headed down Lake Winnipeg for York Factory with the HBC factor. Robertson caught up with them at Jack River House near the north end of the lake. The factor chose John Clarke to take over leadership of the Athabasca expedition and asked Robertson to conduct the colonists back to the Red River and to assist them in re-establishing the colony. Despite his reservations about Clarke's leadership abilities and his disinclination to lead the colonists, Robertson felt he had no option but to agree to the factor's request because he needed the Red River colony to provide provisions for the Athabasca traders.

Re-establishment of the Red River Settlement
Robertson quickly got the colony up and running again. Then he launched a war of nerves against the NWC over the winter. He raided Fort Gibraltar, where he seized some documents that convinced him another NWC attack on the colony was imminent. As a result, he arrested one of the NWC leaders. Robertson tried to convince Governor Semple of the risk of another attack, but Semple refused to take Robertson's warnings seriously.

Robertson argued that Semple—whom he persistently called "Mr. Simple" in letters to him—should keep the colonists together at the fort until the danger was over. "Crush our opponents! Establish the Colony! Then adopt what measures you think most conducive to the interest of the Earl of Selkirk," he wrote.

The day after sending that message, Robertson had decided to leave the settlement. "I had rather be anywhere, than where I am. At the same time it grieves me to leave the Colony at this particular crisis. I wish to God I had never seen it!" Shortly after leaving, Robertson had cooled down sufficiently that he turned back and sent a truculent note reoffering his services to Semple. Not surprisingly, Semple rejected this offer. The events of June 19, nine days after Robertson left the colony, proved his fears to have been well-founded. The Battle of Seven Oaks took place that day, and 21 men, including Semple, were killed.

Robertson attempted to return to England that autumn. He caught the company ship at York Factory in September, but it was blocked by ice in October, and he had to spend the winter in the North. When he learned in the spring that he was to be arraigned in Montreal for his attacks on Fort Gibraltar, he journeyed overland to Montreal immediately to present himself for trial, even though he had not received a formal summons to do so. When he arrived in Montreal in August 1817, he refused to accept bail and insisted on going to prison because he was anxious to stand trial as soon as possible. The case was heard in spring 1818, and Robertson was acquitted.

Athabasca Disaster

John Clarke worked for the NWC between 1800 and 1810, spending some time in the Athabasca country before returning to his birthplace of Montreal. Later that year he became a partner in John Jacob Astor's Pacific Fur Company. During the War of 1812, the Pacific Fur Company was sold to the NWC, so Clarke returned to work with the NWC until Robertson hired him for the HBC.

The Athabasca expedition faced difficulties almost from the time Clarke took charge of it in the early fall of 1815. It soon ran short of food because he had refused to carry any pemmican. In October, Clarke established Fort Wedderburn on an island in Lake Athabasca and took five canoes up the Peace River. Then the expedition met with disaster. The Nor'Westers succeeded in cutting off Clarke's food supplies by using their power to prevent local First Nations people from trading either furs or food with him. Although Clarke pledged his personal property for some food, 16 men starved to death. Not only did the expedition end with a tragic loss of life, but the great expenses incurred were not even partially compensated for by a good return in furs.

Although Clarke barely survived, he was eager to return to Athabasca the following year. The HBC's London Committee, unaware of the disaster and Clarke's apparent incompetence as a leader, gave him command again. In January 1817, a NWC partner and justice of the peace imprisoned Clarke and his officers and seized their fort. Clarke was released on security, but his trade goods were taken, and he lost the respect of the First Nations people in whose presence he had been arrested.

After hearing what had happened, Robertson praised Clarke's courage but noted that "the heroic manner he bore his misfortunes covers a multitude of sins." Later, after learning about Clarke's arrest by the NWC, he wrote that Clarke's "inordinate vanity is such that the management of John Clarke is as arduous a task as that of opposing the NWC."

Despite continuing widespread criticism of Clarke and his methods, he was not fired and continued to work for the HBC until the mid-1830s. In 1831, he visited London to seek HBC recognition for his past services because "to the joint efforts of Mr. Robertson and myself are the HBC in a great measure indebted for the splendour and importance of their rank and standing in the great commercial world." The HBC governor commented that the London Committee "treated him with the contempt he deserved."

Robertson Goes to the Athabasca Country

Immediately after his trial in 1818, Robertson agreed to establish the HBC in Athabasca himself. Norway House on Lake Winnipeg became the centre of the HBC transportation

Lieutenant George Back painted this view of the Hudson's Bay Company and North West Company forts at Île-à-la-Crosse in 1820.
LIBRARY AND ARCHIVES CANADA C-145919

system. Robertson commanded 26 officers and 160 men in a district that stretched from Île-à-la-Crosse to Lesser Slave Lake. He arrived at Fort Wedderburn in the fall of 1818, almost a month before the Nor'Westers, for whom he had arranged a series of "mischances" to delay them at portages. Before the Nor'Westers arrived, Robertson was able to regain the trust of at least some of the First Nations people.

The two opposing groups of fur traders harassed each other daily after the NWC men arrived. The Nor'Westers visited Fort Wedderburn every evening and challenged Robertson's men to come out and fight. According to Robertson, "A little Frenchman of ours" accepted a challenge from one of the NWC "bullies" and gave him "an unmerciful thrashing." Robertson also optimistically reported that "the Indians have regained confidence in us and boldly leave the Nor'Westers every day for the Hudson's Bay." Shortly after this, however, the NWC arrested Robertson at gunpoint and took him to Fort Chipewyan, where he remained a prisoner for the rest of the winter. Robertson described his arrival at Fort Chipewyan:

> I dashed for their Indian hall and at once . . . called on the Indians, representing that the cowardly attack was an effort to reduce them to slavery; but Black [the Nor'Wester who had arrested him] rushed up to stop me. Seizing a fork on the hall table I kept the vagabond at bay. I loaded him with every abuse and evil name I could think of . . . [Then I said to the Indians], do not abandon the Hudson's Bay on this account! There are brave men at our fort to protect you.

In the spring of 1819, while being taken to Fort William by the NWC brigade, Robertson escaped. As they were passing Cumberland House, Robertson asked if he could stop there to say goodbye to his colleagues. The Nor'Westers agreed, but once Robertson was inside the fort, he bolted the doors and refused to come out. The angry Nor'Westers had to continue on without him. Shortly afterwards, seven NWC partners were captured by the new governor-in-chief of Rupert's Land at Grand Rapids on the Saskatchewan. Accompanied by Robertson, the governor took his prisoners to York Factory.

The very characteristics that made Robertson invaluable in the campaign against the Nor'Westers—his generosity (with other people's money), his ability as a salesman and his love of dramatic action—made him ineffectual in routine work where ability in bargaining and accounting were important. He lost the support of the HBC London Committee and was not directly involved with the amalgamation of the NWC and HBC. The head of the new company, Governor George Simpson, characterized Robertson as "a frothy conceited man, who would starve in any other country and is perfectly useless here . . . his integrity is very questionable. To the fur trade he is quite a . . . heavy burden . . . a compound of folly and extravagance."

Robertson conceded that he was extravagant, but he was convinced that extravagance was sometimes necessary. As he put it, "Glittering pomposity has an amazing effect on the freemen, Métis, and Indians." He also was not an easy person to get along with and admitted to a hasty temper, saying, "When you are among wolves, howl!"

Willard-Ferdinand Wentzel

Son of a Norwegian-born merchant in Montreal, Willard-Ferdinand Wentzel became a NWC clerk in 1799 and spent most of his life in Athabasca country, where he became friends with Roderick McKenzie, who had constructed Fort Chipewyan on Lake Athabasca in 1788. Apparently a very intelligent man and a good trader, he made few friends due to his love of sarcasm and pointing out people's weaknesses. This may have contributed to his limited promotion within the company. He was also an excellent musician who collected voyageur songs, which McKenzie described as "mostly obscene and unfit for publication."

In a letter written to a friend in the spring of 1818, Wentzel reported optimistically on the Athabasca trade. He claimed that trade had gone up by nearly 50 packs of furs over the previous year, while the HBC "have not even a half pack to boast of." Commenting on Colin Robertson, who was en route to Athabasca at this time, he concluded that "there is every likelihood of a strong struggle this ensuing season; but everyone here seems to behold this formidable appearance with cool contempt."

Wentzel was hired by Sir John Franklin during the famous explorer's first Arctic trip in 1819. That spring, Simon McGillivray wrote to tell all the NWC agents that both the NWC and the HBC had agreed that their employees would offer every assistance to Franklin. McGillivray assured them that Franklin's expedition "was of a purely public and scientific nature and has no connection whatever with any disputes or territorial claims in discussion between us and the Hudson's Bay Company." The British government promised to pay the fur-trade companies for any supplies obtained or men hired from them by Franklin. Wentzel described his job as being "to settle the Indians required for leaders, guides and hunters." He accompanied Franklin only as far as the Arctic Ocean. By this time, the expedition was so short of provisions that Franklin sent Wentzel back to Great Bear Lake for food. Wentzel found neither game nor hunters there or at Great Slave Lake. Wisely, he did not attempt to rejoin the Franklin party because it lost 11 out of 20 men over the next three years. Most died of starvation, and at least one man was murdered. Franklin perished on his third Arctic expedition in 1847.

Wentzel left Athabasca country for Canada in 1825 and worked for the HBC on the St. Lawrence River for several years before dying of cholera in 1832.

10

Garry and McGillivray: The End of the North West Company

Such of them as are married have the wisdom to retire to their own house; but the bachelors . . . eat, drink and play away as long as the goods hold out; and when these are gone, they even sell their . . . clothes. This done, they are forced upon a new voyage for subsistence.

—WASHINGTON IRVING'S DESCRIPTION OF VOYAGEURS
CELEBRATING THEIR RETURN TO MONTREAL

William McGillivray

"They're here! The canoes are back!" Everyone in Montreal seemed to be shouting these words, either in French or in

English. Soon almost every male—except the very oldest and youngest—and many of the younger women were hurrying down the rough trail between Montreal and Lachine, where the first of the brigade of 20 or 30 canoes were landing. Everyone was trying to be first to greet relatives and friends whom they hadn't seen for many months or even years. By evening, Montreal was in full festival mode. The streets thronged with people eating, drinking and dancing. Church bells were ringing and flags were flying.

Ox carts loaded with furs from the canoes made their way from Lachine to Montreal. Many of these furs were going to Simon McTavish's warehouse. It was the summer of 1783, and McTavish's nephew William McGillivray, newly arrived from Scotland, was quickly caught up in the excitement. The next day, William would begin his fur-trade career by helping to unpack the furs.

Forty years later, McGillivray recalled his arrival in Montreal and his first posting to fur-trade country, or le pays d'en haut, as the Canadians called it. He also recalled another trip to Lachine 15 years later in 1798 and a lunch hosted by Alexander Mackenzie and himself—just one of the many memorable parties held there. All but one of the men in attendance were Scottish Highlanders by birth, so naturally the bottle circulated freely with numerous *dioch* and *dorich* (a drink at the door or farewell drink) and Highland reminiscences. The party did not end until nearly 9 PM, when Mackenzie and McGillivray finally slid off their chairs, joining the other guests on the floor. The only non-Highlander guest, a young military engineer named George Landmann, wrote that by six or seven o'clock he had, in common with many of the others, "fallen from my seat." In order to protect himself from being trampled, he crawled into an empty fireplace where he stayed until the party broke up.

McGillivray also remembered proudly that he was the first English (meaning English-speaking) clerk engaged in the service of the NWC. In 1804, on the death of his uncle, Simon McTavish, he had become the head of the NWC. Now, in 1821, his brother Simon (representing the NWC) and Nicholas Garry (representing the HBC) were going to preside over the official end of the NWC, which was amalgamating with the HBC. It was a sad end to his life's work. The McGillivrays did not actually realize—or perhaps they just didn't admit—how serious the situation was becoming for their company until late in 1820. Simon then took a leading role in merging the two fur-trade companies. In March 1821, negotiations were completed, and Simon was in Montreal two months later, working to get the agreement accepted by the Nor'Westers.

William accompanied Simon and Garry as far as Fort William, where they would meet with the wintering partners at the final NWC rendezvous. The winterers listened silently to William's report on the terms of the agreement signed by the two companies, then burst into shouts of indignation. They feared many would be left unemployed, and they wondered how those who didn't lose their jobs would be able to work with their former enemies. They also realized that Montreal would no longer be a major player in the fur trade.

"Amalgamation, this is not amalgamation. This is submersion. We are drowned men!" one winterer said bitterly. Much too late they realized the price they were paying for their strong individuality. Had they remained united, they might have won much better terms during the negotiations leading up to the amalgamation. When the meeting ended, William sadly returned to Montreal. Due to his poor health, he was not going to accompany Simon and Garry on their inspection trip from Fort William to York Factory.

Colin Robertson wrote on July 12, 1821, that "Simon McGillivray has carried everything without even the semblance of opposition. The first day he opened the business, the second the deed and release was signed, and the third all the peace and harmony." This obviously was not true. Perhaps Robertson really believed it, but it is more likely that he chose not to acknowledge how the Nor'Westers really felt.

Nicholas Garry

Nicholas Garry, a member of the HBC London Committee, had volunteered to travel from Montreal to York Factory with Simon McGillivray to do whatever was needed to implement the merger agreement between the HBC and the NWC. In the detailed diary Garry kept of his trip, he described his first meeting with McGillivray:

> But a few months before, Mr. McGillivray, with whom I am to travel so many thousand miles, with whom I have to arrange so many points of importance affecting the happiness and fortune of so many people, [was only] known to me . . . as the most active and strenuous opposer of the interests of the company I came out to represent . . . [At our first meeting] a simultaneous movement brought our hands together, and if the feeling was not a true one, an intention to act fairly, kindly considerately by each other, there is more hypocrisy in the world than appears to me to be possible.

This good feeling did not last very long. At the end of their three weeks of meetings in Fort William, Garry wrote that "never in my life have I left a place with less regret."

In early August, Garry and Simon McGillivray arrived at Bas de la Rivière on Lake Winnipeg. Garry thought the post was in a beautiful location and noted approvingly that they were growing potatoes, wheat and vegetables there. He noted with disapproval, however, that there were 50 women and children living at the post at company expense and that "some steps should be taken to avoid it." Next day, "being anxious on many accounts" not to arrive at the Red River with McGillivray, Garry ordered his canoe to set off at 6 AM, feeling "much relief" in being without his travel companion.

A few days later, Garry arrived at the camp of Ojibwa Chief Peguis. Peguis and his people had offered help to the settlers at the time of the Battle of Seven Oaks, so Simon refused to stop there. According to Garry, William McGillivray had told Peguis he was a bad person for having defended the colony; therefore Simon would have nothing to do with him. Peguis had a Union Jack hoisted with the HBC arms given to him by Selkirk. He showed Garry a testimonial written on moose hide saying that the chief had always been a faithful, sincere friend of the colony and recommending him to the attentions of the officers of the HBC.

Garry's canoe got caught in a storm on Lake Winnipeg and scarcely made it safely to shore. When he landed, Garry saw that McGillivray was still out on the lake and evidently did not plan to seek shelter. McGillivray finally came ashore just as the storm became even worse. While Garry admitted that McGillivray's canoe was larger than his and could better stand the high waves, he still criticized McGillivray's behaviour:

> We learnt afterwards that the standing out was only bravado, wishing us first to encamp that they might have the opportunity to vaunt their prowess. Miserable vanity, which might have cost the lives of many brave people, who protested against the step. The steersman was actually changed [for] refusing to conduct the canoe. The history of his vanity was that after an attempt at Fort William to give me a weak

crew and a bad canoe, it was a source of great annoyance that we led the march.

On August 23, Garry and McGillivray arrived at York Factory shortly after two ships from England. One ship carried 170 colonists from Switzerland. Garry said that two Canadians from McGillivray's canoe "were poisoning the minds" of the new colonists. Both Garry and the HBC governor ordered the two men out of the camp, but they refused to go, saying that Garry was not their bourgeois. Garry consulted with McGillivray, but "instead of at once ordering them off, he reasoned with them and even took their part."

On September 14, 1821, Garry set sail on *Prince of Wales* to return to England. He summarized his trip as he was leaving, saying that he thought "all parties satisfied and united except those who have sinister and sordid views to carry into effect (which I have had the advantage to unmask) and having had it in my power to protect so many people who otherwise would have suffered."

Epilogue

WILLIAM MCGILLIVRAY DIED IN 1825, and the family company was declared bankrupt shortly afterwards. Simon McGillivray, who lived until 1840, no longer had any connection with the fur trade.

What of the other Nor'Westers? Some continued their employment with the HBC, and life changed very little for them. Others, however, either lost their jobs or refused to work for a company that they considered the enemy. Of these, some retired, others took up farming as John Pritchard had done, and still others became free traders.

Although the NWC name disappeared after 1821, it was revived 170 years later. In the mid-1980s, the HBC had 178 northern stores, most of which were former trading posts.

Epilogue

At that time, a group of investors purchased the Northern Stores Division from the HBC and in 1990 formally renamed it the North West Company. The HBC stopped buying furs in 1991, although the new NWC continues to market furs.

Although few people make their living as trappers today, and many people would like to see trapping outlawed, some people continue to trap at least part-time. The Manitoba Trappers Association organizes an event known as the Thompson Fur Table every year in mid-December. Trappers from all over the North gather in Thompson to market their furs, visit and go shopping—just as their ancestors would have done at places like Michilimackinac and Fort William over two centuries ago.

Fur-Trade Timeline

Late 16th century The fur trade began almost as soon as the first Europeans arrived in northern North America, when Native people brought furs to trade at fishing stations on the St. Lawrence River and in Acadia.

1600 The French government granted a fur-trade monopoly to Pontgravé and Sieur De Monts.

1608 Samuel de Champlain established a base at Quebec.

1615 Champlain reached Lake Nipissing and Georgian Bay.

1668 French explorers and fur traders Radisson and Des Groseilliers travelled to Hudson Bay, where they hoped to establish a trading base. When the French would not back their plans, they successfully approached the English.

1670 The Hudson's Bay Company received a Royal Charter granting it control over all lands draining into Hudson Bay. It began by trading furs from posts on the shores of Hudson and James bays with the help of Native middlemen.

Late 17th century French traders controlled the Great Lakes, upper Mississippi and Ohio Valleys from Quebec; British colonies controlled the areas to the south, and the HBC controlled areas to the north and west.

1756–63 The Seven Years War (known as the French and Indian War in North America) took place. The British defeated the French and their Native allies. New France capitulated after the fall of Montreal in 1760; however, the war did not officially end until the signing of the Treaty of Paris in 1763.

Mid-1770s The North West Company was organized, with Simon McTavish as the head.

1775 Samuel Hearne built the first inland HBC post at Cumberland House on the Saskatchewan River.

1782 The French captured Fort Prince of Wales and York Factory from the British and destroyed them; however, the British almost immediately regained control.

1784 William McGillivray began his apprenticeship with NWC.

1798 The XY or New North West Company was formed, which rejoined the NWC in 1804.

1804 Simon McTavish died, and his nephew William McGillivray replaced him as head of the NWC.

1812 The Red River Settlement was established by Lord Selkirk.

1812 The War of 1812 broke out.

1816 The conflict between the NWC and the HBC over the Red River Settlement culminated in the Battle of Seven Oaks.

1821 The NWC and the HBC were amalgamated.

Selected Bibliography

Bumsted, J.M. *Fur Trade Wars: The Founding of Western Canada.*
Winnipeg: Great Plains Publications, 1999.

Campbell, Marjorie Wilkins. *The Saskatchewan: the Great Rivers of
Canada.* Toronto: Clarke, Irwin, 1950.

Chaboillez, Charles. "The Journal of Charles Jean-Baptiste Chaboillez,
1797–1798." Edited by Harold Hickerson. *Ethnohistory* 6, no. 3
(Summer 1959): 265–316, and no. 4 (Autumn 1959): 363–427.

Cocking, Matthew. *An Adventure from Hudson Bay.* Edited by
Lawrence Burpee. Ottawa: Royal Society of Canada, 1908. Also at
http://peel.library.ualberta.ca.

Dictionary of Canadian Biography Online. www.biographi.ca.

Garry, Nicholas. *Diary of Nicholas Garry, deputy-governor of the
Hudson's Bay Company from 1822-1835.* Ottawa: Royal Society of
Canada, 1900. Also at http://peel.library.ualberta.ca.

Gates, Charles M., ed. *Five Fur Traders of the Northwest.* Introduction
by Grace Lee Nute. Minneapolis: University of Minnesota Press,
1933. Also at http://peel.library.ualberta.ca.

Graham, Andrew. *Andrew Graham's Observations on Hudson's Bay
1767-1791.* London: Hudson's Bay Record Society, Vol. XXVII
(available from HBC Archives).

Hearne, Samuel. *A Journey from Prince of Wales's Fort.* London:
Strathan and Cadell, 1795. Reprint, Toronto: Champlain Society,
1911. Also at http://peel.library.ualberta.ca.

Henry, Alexander (the Elder). *Travels and Adventures in Canada and
the Indian Territories between the Years 1760 and 1776.* New York:
I. Riley, 1809. Also at http://www.canadiana.org.

Selected Bibliography

Innis, Harold A. *Peter Pond: Fur Trader and Adventurer.* Toronto: Irwin
& Gordon, 1930. Also at www.gutenberg.ca.

Irving, Washington. *Astoria.* Paris: Baudry's European Library, 1836.
Also at www.history1700s.com/etext/html/blstria10.shtml.

Johnson, Alice M., ed. *Saskatchewan Journals and Correspondence:
Edmonton House 1795-1800, Chesterfield House 1800-1802.*
London: Hudson's Bay Record Society, 1967.

Landmann, George Thomas. *Adventures and Recollections of Colonel
Landmann Late of the Corps of Royal Engineers.* Vol. 1. London:
Colburn & Co., 1852. Also at http://babel.hathitrust.org.

Mackenzie, Alexander. *First Man West: Alexander Mackenzie's Journal
of His Voyage to the Pacific Coast of Canada in 1793.* Edited by
Walter Sheppe. Montreal: McGill University Press, 1962.

———. *Voyages from Montreal on the River St. Laurence, through the
Continent of North America.* London: Cadell and Davis, 1801. Also
at http://peel.library.ualberta.ca.

Masson, L.R., ed. *Les Bourgeois de la Compagnie du Nord-Ouest.* 2 vols.
Quebec: A. Coté et Cie., 1889–90. Also at http://www.canadiana.org.

McGillivray, Duncan. *The Journal of Duncan M'Gillivray.*
Edited by A.S. Morton. Toronto: Macmillan, 1929. Also at
http://peel.library.ualberta.ca.

McGillivray, Simon. *The North West Company in Rebellion.* Edited
by Jean Morrison. Thunder Bay: Thunder Bay Historical Museum
Society, 1988.

Newman, Peter C. *Company of Adventurers.* Markham: Penguin Books,
1985.

———. *Caesars of the Wilderness.* Markham: Penguin Books, 1987.

Pritchard, John. *Narratives of John Pritchard.* London: John Murray,
1819. Also at http://peel.library.ualberta.ca.

Rich, E.E. *The Fur Trade and the Northwest to 1857.* Toronto:
McClelland & Stewart, 1967.

Robertson, Colin. *Colin Robertson's Correspondence Book, Sept. 1817 to Sept. 1822.* Edited by E.E. Rich. Toronto: Champlain Society, 1939. Also at http://www.champlainsociety.ca.

Sutherland, Donna. *Nahoway: a Distant Voice.* Petersfield, MB: White Buffalo Books, 2008.

Tanner, John. *Narrative of the Captivity and Adventures of John Tanner.* London: Baldwin & Cradock, 1830. Also at http://peel.library.ualberta.ca.

Thompson, David. *David Thompson's Narrative of His Explorations in Western America, 1784–1812.* Edited by Richard Glover. Toronto: Champlain Society, 1962. Also at http://www.champlainsociety.ca.

———. *Travels in Western North America 1784-1812.* Edited by Victor G. Hopwood. Toronto: Macmillan of Canada, 1971.

Wallace, W. Stewart, ed. *Documents Relating to the North West Company.* Toronto: The Champlain Society, 1934. Also at http://www.champlainsociety.ca.

White, Bruce M. *Grand Portage as a Trading Post.* Grand Marais, Minnesota: Grand Portage National Monument, 2005. Also at www.nps.gov/history/history/online_books/grpo1/fur_trade.pdf.

Index

Acknowledgements

Thank you to the following for their assistance:

My husband, Don, who contributed to the map for this book and provided helpful comments on the text.

A friend, Berthe La Flèche, who helped me translate some French material.

Editor Lesley Reynolds, who did an excellent job of preparing my manuscript for publication. Working with Lesley was a pleasure because we were almost always in agreement about what changes needed to be made.

A fellow Manitoba writer and friend, Donna Sutherland, whose book *Nahoway: a Distant Voice* provided the information about her ancestors William Sinclair and Nahoway that I included in chapter 6.

About the Author

Irene Ternier Gordon was raised on a grain farm in west-central Saskatchewan and has lived along the historic Assiniboine River just west of Winnipeg since 1989. She has been interested in western-Canadian history since she was 11 years old and first read the children's historical novels written by Manitoban Olive Knox. Irene began her writing career in 1998, after working as a teacher-librarian for 15 years. When she is not writing, she is an avid traveller and especially enjoys going someplace warm for a couple of weeks every winter. She also likes to hike, ski and spend time with family and friends.

People of the Fur Trade is Irene's seventh book. For more information about Irene or her work, please go to www.ireneterniergordon.ca or contact her at author@ireneterniergordon.ca.